Contents

preface

▶ I remember lying in a hospital bed, muted light filtering in through the blinds, marvelling that I was still alive. I thought of my precious newborn daughter and wondered how on earth I was going to look after her when I wasn't sure I could look after myself. It wasn't like I didn't want to be here any more, it was more of a question of how I was going to muster the energy or the strength to keep going.

This time in my life, when I felt energetically bankrupt, was precisely the moment that I was called upon to step up like never before. Any parent will attest to that challenge of caring for a newborn. And similarly, at a time when I needed my parents like never before, I was losing my father, and for a time, my mother too. My dad was lying in his own hospital bed, fighting for every breath. My mother was a stalwart by his side, his advocate when he was unable to speak for himself, and there she remained for months.

I felt cracked open like a nut, completely laid bare and utterly fragmented. The world felt like

the self-care revolution

smart habits & simple practices to allow you to flourish

Suzy Reading

aster

a profoundly different place and I knew I was in some kind of transition, but one I didn't know how to navigate. I needed someone to help me make sense of these feelings, and I voiced that need. A bearded man was sent in to assess me for risk of self-harm or being a danger to my child. This started what I felt was a disappointing journey with the medical system.

It wasn't that the man lacked compassion, it was just that my cry for help wasn't met with what I needed. A kind ear, warm understanding and some words of encouragement would've gone a long way. Someone to give me permission to feel as I was feeling, to say 'of course you feel this way'. It took me a long time to find the kind of support I really needed. If this feels close to home, please keep looking. I hope this book will be a tonic for you.

I don't know whether it was exhaustion, grief, postnatal depression or a combination of those things. In a lot of ways, I don't think a label is even necessary, I was just having a normal, human response to an extremely taxing set of variables. Whatever it was, I really struggled.

My husband and I had just moved back from the UK to my family home in Sydney to be closer to my parents and to start a family of our own. We'd had a very worrying year with my father and we all knew something was seriously wrong. An esteemed doctor himself, Dad had been investigating the possible causes of his marked ageing and fatigue. No answers had been found. One evening, he looked so grey I gently asked him if he would consider going

to hospital. He declined, accepting that he would go in the morning. A few hours later, Mum tapped on my bedroom door saying she had called the paramedics. I went downstairs to find Dad in bed, hardly breathing, twitching from the deprivation of oxygen. I took his hand and all I could do was reassure him that we were by his side and that help was on its way. With the heightened sensitivity of being 40 weeks pregnant, bearing witness to that event understandably had an indelible effect on me and my nervous system.

With my husband and mother, I sat outside the resuscitation room, in the same hospital I was due to give birth in, waiting to hear if my father would survive this breathing failure. The paramedics had told us it was unlikely he would make it to hospital alive, and like a stunned mullet, I waited there until the early hours of the morning, when a nurse softly suggested

I go home and rest. Truthfully, my own health and the prospect of giving birth was far from my mind; I was completely absorbed in the crisis at hand.

Amazingly, my father rallied and, though in a coma and on a breathing machine, he survived. Doctors couldn't explain his breathing failure, and we didn't know whether he would regain consciousness or even what faculties he would possess if he did. It was a long and agonizing week of 'last goodbyes' before I went into labour, delivering my firstborn, Charlotte Rose. The act of giving birth after a time of such emotional turmoil took every ounce of strength I possessed. I began life as a mother at energetic rock bottom – traumatized and deeply sad.

My dad spent the next four months in intensive care, enduring invasive tests and procedures, none of which yielded a diagnosis or hope of treatment. The early months of Charlotte's life revolved around making hospital visits, and there was little light relief. After months of tending to my father's needs at the expense of her own, my mother was hospitalized with cellulitis, an infection which left untreated can rapidly turn life threatening. So, for a few weeks there, I had a baby with reflux who didn't sleep for more than a few hours at a stretch and both parents in different hospitals, needing different things. That experience honestly nearly broke me. Thankfully, my mum made a full recovery. My father gradually reclaimed the ability to breathe on his own while awake and the ability to walk. After weeks of intensive work in a rehabilitation unit though, it was clear that he was never going to be well enough to come home.

Given the high level of care my dad needed, there were few facilities available to him and he ended up in a care home we never felt comfortable with, but there were no other options. It was the kind of place where you knew the residents weren't going anywhere else, and I found that deeply depressing. People used to come out of the woodwork when I brought Charlotte to visit – a bouncing baby was simply irresistible, a transfusion of light and life, but it wasn't the kind of place you wanted to take your child.

This chapter was characterized by deep guilt – that Dad was there in the first place and about not wanting to be there either. In truth, I just wanted this suffering to be over. The reality of that statement overwhelmed me with guilt. I recount this part of my journey not to depress you or to elicit your sympathy. It's that I have encountered so many people since who've been through similar experiences and my message is simple – give yourself permission to think and feel as you do. It doesn't make you a bad person, it makes you human. The guilt you pile on yourself you neither need nor deserve. Please go gently on you.

Witnessing the agonizing decline of my father completely dominated the first chapter of Charlotte's life. You can't split your psyche in two. I couldn't simultaneously grieve for my father and celebrate the new life of my daughter. Quite simply, grief won out. With no diagnosis and therefore no treatment, it was just a painful wait. He was there, but just a shadow of himself and with such a diminished quality of life. Still fighting for every breath and to complete the smallest of daily tasks. You wouldn't wish it on your

worst enemy. He finally passed away when Charlotte was fifteen months old and was posthumously diagnosed as having a rare variant of motor neurone disease – nothing would have saved him. My father's freedom from suffering was a profound relief and it provided the space for the healing to begin. The one silver lining in all this was that he had met Charlotte Rose and seen his granddaughter blossom.

During those fifteen months, under the weight of all that distress, I felt like my nervous system was completely fried. I was constantly on edge, teary, quick to anger, and highly sensitive to noise and stimulation. I had begun to isolate myself socially – conversation felt difficult, and in my head, it was impossible to make plans with an unsettled baby. The constant thought running through my mind was

'how am I going to continue?' I made repeat visits to my doctor asking for help with my exhaustion and low mood. I was given what I felt were two disappointing options – take antidepressants to help me cope better, or minimize the stress in my life. I couldn't stop mothering or extricate myself from my father's care and I didn't want to alter my brain chemistry when I felt I was having a normal, human reaction to an intense set of circumstances.

Thankfully, I found a middle path. As a psychologist and yoga teacher I knew there were options, I just lacked the energy to carve that path on my own. Working with a postnatal depression counsellor I was introduced for the first time to the term 'self-care'. I was instantly intrigued and couldn't fathom how in six years of psychology education I had never encountered it. Even now when you Google 'self-care' you are likely to find tips on how to adhere to your medication regime. From my own healing journey and now in my role as a well-being psychologist, I have come to see self-care as so much more. Self-care is proactive healthcare. I see it as the future of preventative medicine and the route to feeling whole, healthy, happy and the best version of myself. While self-care was enough to get me back on my feet, it is very important to note that there is a valid time and place for antidepressant medication, which can be just the tonic to help people when they need it most and necessary in the management of some conditions. Self-care can be an additional means to feeling better, not necessarily an alternative.

My counsellor opened my eyes to seeing self-care as a way of nourishing myself, rebuilding my energy stores so that I could weather and heal from the storm of stress I was in. It wasn't going to remove the pain, but it was going to give me the ability to cope better and carry on. First, she encouraged me to think about all the things I used to do to nurture myself. Most of these things had dropped away because I was flat out or too tired, and many were simply no longer accessible to me because of my changed life circumstances. Those walks on the beach, movies with mates, yoga classes and spa days felt like a different lifetime. We took a look together at what I could realistically reintegrate into my life and considered new avenues of replenishment.

Gradually, I got back on my yoga mat, even if it was just to lie there. I took a daily 'mindful' walk rather than a 'ruminating' one. I started reading uplifting books again and deliberately avoided life-sapping activities. I took a break from watching the evening news, which can be toxic to a depressed mind and body. This was enough to cultivate a shift in my energy and a noticeable shift in my thinking.

It sparked my passion for self-care and the desire to empower others with these tools to reclaim their health and well-being. This is why I am writing this book – to share these strategies with you, in the hope that they can build you back up so you can carry on and to best prepare you for the rollercoaster of life.

So, even psychologists get the blues...maybe that's a no-brainer to you. Great! I figure if it can normalize how just one person feels, then it is worth saying. Learning that our feelings are normal provides us with an opportunity to heal. No one is immune from stress, fatigue, an inner critic, or what I see as an accumulation of tragedies as we grow older – we all lose people we love, we all have a fallible mind and body. If you are feeling at a low ebb, you are not alone. I have been there too, clawed my way back to vitality and I want to share with you that toolkit.

What we need are micro moments of nurturing dotted throughout our days. That's what this book is about – empowering you with your own bespoke Self-Care Toolkit, helping you navigate stress, loss and change, promoting healing, protecting you from burnout, cultivating clarity and maximizing life's joys. Read on my friend, we're in it together.

If you are feeling at a low ebb, know you are not alone. I have been there too, I have clawed my way back to vitality and I want to share with you that toolkit.

INTRODUCTION TO SELF-CARE

▶ A few years ago during a visit to see my husband's family in the UK, it became apparent to us that my father-in-law was seriously unwell. Having had the privilege of being with my father during his last chapter, I didn't want my husband to miss out on that precious time. So we went back home to Australia, packed up our Sydney life and moved back to the UK, all while expecting our second child. We thought we would have years to enjoy together – it turned out to be just months and again we were thrown back into that space of mourning the passing of life while trying to celebrate a new one.

Embarking on that move, we knew it was going to be hard. And it was tough, even more painful and achingly tiring than I had anticipated. But this time around I didn't fall down. At no point during all the turmoil did I stop wanting to be here on this earth. Yes, I had a different head on my shoulders, yes, every baby is different, but the primary reason for my greater resilience in the midst of those crazy challenges was down to regular self-care.

WHAT IS SELF-CARE?

▸ Self-care is any life-giving activity that restores, sustains or improves your health. In the simplest of terms, I think of self-care as nourishment. Most people will mention things like facials, dinners out and holidays when asked what they consider to be self-care. Of course they are one hundred per cent right, but self-care is so much more.

The challenge with the activities that come to mind for most people is that they can be costly, time consuming and they need to be booked in advance, making them difficult to access in times of genuine need. This book will show you many ways to replenish that take little time, energy or expense. Simple mood boosters, like wearing your favourite colour or spritzing your favourite scent, or effortless ways to relax, like lying down with your legs up against the wall for five minutes or watching the moving cloudscape for a few moments.

Self-care helps people become the best version of themselves.

YOUR ENERGETIC BANK BALANCE

▶ When introducing self-care to my clients, I like to use the concept of us all having an 'energy bank balance'. Like a car needs petrol to go, we need energy to get us through our day. Self-care is like refuelling your tank – each activity is a deposit in our energy bank. We need a healthy energy bank balance just to sustain us through the usual demands of life. If you are just scraping by with the status quo of life, how are you going to cope when life throws a curveball at you? You or someone in your care falls ill and you're up all night, work becomes difficult, you have an accident or you get a promotion – curveballs can be positive too! Even much desired happenings can tax us too, such as planning a holiday, moving houses or starting a family. Because stress is an unavoidable part of life I think it makes more sense to manage our energetic reserves rather than attempting to manage our stress. When we are feeling full of vigour and in great health we naturally deal better with stress. Commitment to regular self-care gives you the best possible chance to cope with all the challenges that come your way.

Another image I like to use is 'filling your cup'. When people talk of feeling selfish about taking time out for themselves, the image of a cup is helpful. You can't pour from an empty cup, so replenishing yourself is the only way to ensure your ability to keep giving. Another metaphor is to think of self-care in the same way as the oxygen masks on a plane in the case of an emergency. For the safety of all in your care, you must ensure your mask is fitted first before you can attend to those in your charge.

SELF-CARE FOR THE MIND AND BODY

▶ What I have observed in my career as personal trainer, yoga teacher and psychologist is that physical health tends to be high on most people's radar. Public health campaigns have been very effective at promoting the importance of healthy eating, regular exercise, minimizing your intake of alcohol and the need to prioritize adequate sleep.

On the other hand, the strategies we could employ to nourish our mental or emotional health are seen as more luxurious or indulgent. I would love to challenge this. Additionally, the stigma attached to mental health has us saying, 'I'm fine thanks, I don't need that'. I can't tell you how many traumatized people I encounter who say, 'no I don't need help, I'm coping' when they are the prime candidates to benefit from having someone to talk to. I would love to see a shift in public perception that makes caring for your mind as sexy and socially acceptable as working on your 'six pack'. So my mission here is to get you thinking about practices that nurture you mentally, emotionally and energetically.

SELF-CARE ISN'T SELFISH

▶ Often, during periods of stress, loss and change, self-care gets dropped from the agenda. This is precisely when we need it the most – it's exactly what happened to me. Now in my psychological practice I hear my clients saying the same things; they label self-care as 'too hard', 'selfish' or 'an indulgence'. For those that feel it is selfish, take a moment to consider what would happen to the people around you if you fell over. What kind of burden would you place on them if you were unable to keep fulfilling your role? If you can't engage in self-care for yourself, then do it for the people around you. If it helps you, think of self-care not as 'me first', but 'me as well'.

SELF-CARE – WHY WE NEED TO BE PROACTIVE

▸ When the going gets tough it's common to feel
that you just don't have the time, space or energy
for self-care. This is a recipe for full-blown physical
health meltdown, for exhaustion, and if it goes
on for long enough, anxiety and depression. The
World Health Organization predicts that by 2030
depression will be the leading cause of the disease
burden globally[1]. Clearly we cannot afford to be
complacent. You will learn a whole toolkit of self-
care activities in this book that will blow guilt and
other perceived barriers out of the water.

My experience taught me that when we are stressed, our usual methods of replenishment can become inaccessible and we lack the resources to think creatively about carving new self-care rituals. This is why we need to get the concept of self-care into the spotlight, and ideally before we hit energetic rock bottom. We need to talk about it openly with our friends and family. We need to raise awareness of the ways in which we can pay into that energy bank, keeping us resilient in the face of stress. We need to support each other through the challenging times because when you are in the midst of it, the answers can seem hard to find.

What I came to understand through my own experience was that the things I normally and naturally did well, in terms of constructive thought and behaviour patterns, dropped away when I was stressed and exhausted. But the really encouraging thing is that when I committed to self-care these skills bounced back! Similarly, as I empower my clients to take regular action to 'fill their cup', they naturally make better decisions, have more energy to buffer themselves and can engage in more constructive thinking.

WHY DO WE NEED SELF-CARE?

First, let's zoom out and take a look at some facts about stress:

▸ **Stress isn't going to go away.** Stress is a normal part of life. In fact, life would be pretty boring without some stress to keep us on our toes. It's no good saying 'I'll be happy when...' The day when there is no stress is the day we are pushing up daisies.

▸ **Stress has a cumulative effect.** The stress of daily life can all add up and have us reacting inappropriately to minor events – the key is to have regular pressure releases throughout our day to avoid becoming 'Mount Vesuvius'. Putting our heads in the sand and thinking we can just deal with it later wreaks havoc with our health and takes a toll on all aspects of our life.

▸ **Too much stress is dangerous.** Stress lies at the heart of a myriad of physical and mental health conditions. Quite simply, the evidence is overwhelming that too much stress, either in intensity or in duration, makes us ill. We just can't afford to be complacent about our stress levels – too much stress greatly diminishes our ability to enjoy life.

A stress audit of 2,000 UK respondents in 2015 yielded some pretty eye-opening results. A whopping nine out of ten women reported feeling stressed, with 36 per cent agreeing that they were stressed every day. On an encouraging note, over half of respondents stated that taking time to look after their health and well-being is a priority. However, we have a way to go to make self-care an active part of regular life, with 49 per cent of women feeling they don't have enough time to look after themselves. It was these results that catapulted me into action on promoting the tools of self-care, and I have been running fully booked workshops ever since.

HOW DOES SELF-CARE HELP?

▸ **Self-care helps us COPE** during illness, stress, loss and change. I have carers coming to me to help them cope looking after a loved one, parents adjusting to life with a newborn, mothers suffering from postnatal depression, people building a new life after relocating, overworked executives and exam-stressed teenagers.

▸ **Self-care helps us RECOVER** from illness, stress, loss and change. Some of my clients are seeking help after losing a loved one, an experience of betrayal, redundancy, recovering from a range of conditions, including depression, severe illness or after a divorce.

▸ **Self-care offers us a PROTECTIVE FUNCTION,** forming a buffer against future stress. Sometimes, we know a challenge lies ahead and I have worked with some wonderful, proactive people who are preparing themselves for life-changing events and situations. I know that if I had been aware of the concept of self-care I would have chosen differently during that week before the arrival of Charlotte. Had I made different choices, I may not have ended up flat on my back.

▸ **Self-care helps us to FLOURISH as individuals.** In my coaching business, people approach me with a variety of goals. Self-care helps people become the best version of themselves. In this way, I have clients coming to me to help them become the kind of parent or partner they aspire to be, stepping up to embark on a new career, returning to study, seeking a renewed sense of purpose following retirement or simply getting into the shape they want to be in.

BURNOUT

▸ What is burnout? I describe burnout as energetic bankruptcy, and its prevalence is on the rise. Burnout is characterized by exhaustion, manifesting itself emotionally, mentally and physically. It's an overwhelming state, when you feel like you have nothing left to give and you just can't ignore your body's plea for a break.

▸ Prolonged stress or overworking frequently results in a state of burnout. It can be caused by too many burdens coinciding or a cumulative period of stress – where you're hit by one thing after another. Burnout is also caused by relentless pushing, ambition and striving. We render ourselves vulnerable when we neglect our health, burning the candle at both ends as if we are invincible.

Prolonged stress or overworking frequently results in a state of burnout.

What are the signs to look out for?

- Extreme tiredness, trouble sleeping despite feeling fatigued, difficulty switching off and a sense of overstimulation.

- A general suppression of the immune system evidenced by frequent bouts of minor ailments such as cold sores, headaches or common colds, or lingering illnesses.

- Muscular aches, pains and physical tension.

- Low mood, suppressed appetite, poor concentration or diminished enjoyment from life. A sense of feeling stuck and overwhelmed.

- Anxiety, anger, reactivity and irritability. A tendency to generalize about problems, to catastrophize or lose perspective and to take things personally.

Self-care will help heal your system from burnout. If you're constantly feeling overwhelmed, prioritize soothing activities and choices that restore balance to your life. I will guide you through that process. Even if you are not feeling energetically low, engaging in a regular self-care practice will protect you from the ravages of stress, reducing the risk of burnout.

little gems ▸

▸ Stress isn't going to go away, so rather than stress management, let's focus on energy management. Self-care is the way we top up our energetic bank balance, and we are aiming for daily micro moments of nourishment.

▸ Self-care in its simplest definition is nourishment for your head, heart and body.

▸ Self-care boosts our resilience and protects us from burnout and future stresses.

▸ We need self-care to help us cope with and heal from stress, loss and change.

▸ Self-care isn't selfish. If you don't nourish yourself it is very hard to tend well to those in your care. Common perceived barriers to self-care include feelings of guilt (use the mantra: it's not 'me first', it's 'me as well') and feeling that there isn't enough time or energy for it. Engaging in self-care gives you the opportunity to be the person you aspire to be.

notes to myself ›

THE SELF-CARE VITALITY WHEEL

▸ As I started to feel vital and abundant again, I could see how the concept of self-care could be something of great value to others. In fact, for the first time in my career, my disparate qualifications in psychology, fitness and yoga finally seemed to be coming together into a cohesive offering – empowering people with the tools of self-care. I set out to develop a framework that I could easily share, drawing on my own life experiences and qualifications. In particular, this framework is informed by a relatively new branch of psychology called 'Positive Psychology'. This is the study of happiness, well-being and the conditions that make life worth living. The information yielded from research conducted from this discipline is perfect for informing us about how we can harness the power of self-care to maximum effect.

I created the 'Vitality Wheel' as a simple method of communicating the different ways you can make a deposit into your energy bank. The goal of the Vitality Wheel is to empower you to better care for yourself. In one simple diagram you can be reminded of eight different avenues of nourishment.

THE VITALITY WHEEL PATHWAYS ARE:

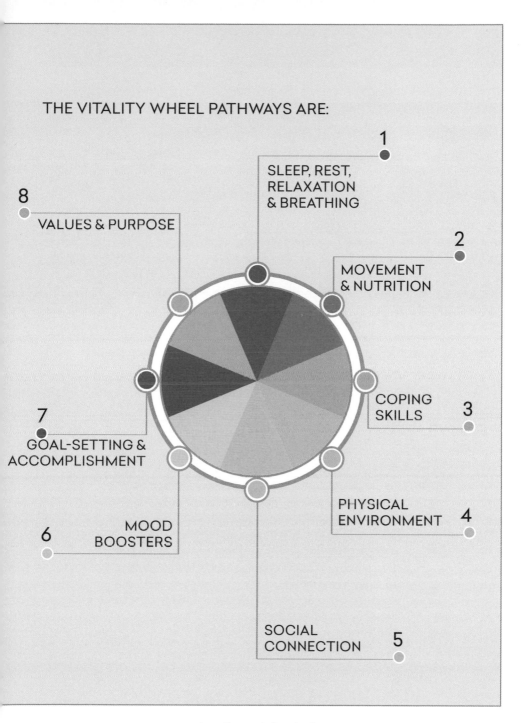

1 SLEEP, REST, RELAXATION & BREATHING

2 MOVEMENT & NUTRITION

3 COPING SKILLS

4 PHYSICAL ENVIRONMENT

5 SOCIAL CONNECTION

6 MOOD BOOSTERS

7 GOAL-SETTING & ACCOMPLISHMENT

8 VALUES & PURPOSE

Some of these might instantly feel familiar and appealing to you, and others might seem rather cryptic and challenging – relax, that's OK! You don't have to address all of these areas, only the ones that feel most resonant. While the Vitality Wheel demonstrates these eight ways to reclaim a sense of energy, balance and calm, there is some overlap between the pathways and they are not intended to be distinct. The point of it is to jog your thinking about what you can do to help yourself right now. Quite often we default to particular types of self-care. For example, when some people feel stressed they habitually turn to exercise as an outlet, so the tips contained in this book might encourage those people to try a different activity or move in a different direction to get a better result.

The Vitality Wheel helps you think more broadly about your nourishment – head, heart and body.

I think it is fair to say that we all know the fundamentals of health and well-being, but many people are not so attuned to the benefits associated with investing in our relationships, the true value of relaxation and sleep, how energizing it is to live a purposeful life or how to employ coping strategies to better navigate stress. The Vitality Wheel helps you think more broadly about your nourishment – head, heart and body. Working your way through the chapters of your choosing, you will be able to build your own personalized collection of self-care activities – your 'Self-Care Toolkit'.

HOW TO USE THIS BOOK

▸ The chapters of this book will take you through each spoke of the Vitality Wheel in finer detail. Each chapter will inspire you with a range of different activities, ideas and affirmations. There are also yoga sequences or movements in each chapter designed to support you as you explore each pathway of the Vitality Wheel.

Work with as many of the Vitality Wheel spokes as you like and feel free to start with reading the chapters that feel most interesting, accessible and replenishing to you. If there are some that don't feel right for you just now, that's fine. This book does not need to be read in chronological order. The ordering of the chapters reflects my personal healing journey; yours might be completely different. If you're ready to make some lifestyle changes, then perhaps you'll want to start with the chapter on goals. If you feel a little bit stuck or are seeking greater clarity, then skip to the chapter on values and purpose. Your interests will naturally change with time, so keep revisiting the book, checking out the Vitality Wheel and thinking about which pathway could work for you now. Consider trying out the yoga sequences from each chapter even if you're not drawn to the other tips and activities.

MAKING A 'MIND MAP' WITH THE VITALITY WHEEL

▸ A mind map is a graphical way to represent ideas and concepts. It is a visual thinking tool that helps you to structure information, to analyze, understand, integrate and recall ideas. Think of the Vitality Wheel as a mind map for self-care. It will help you understand self-care in its true breadth and to recall relevant information in an instant, empowering you to take swift action.

Once you have read a chapter, create a mind map by simply annotating a copy of the Vitality Wheel with the tips, ideas and mantras that spoke to you in that chapter, adding to it as you read on. Hang your personalized wheel somewhere you're likely to see it often, perhaps the fridge or your desk at work. In one glance at your Vitality Wheel you can find something accessible to you in that moment.

BRAINSTORMING YOUR SELF-CARE TOOLKIT

▸ Once you have read a few chapters you can create a Self-Care Toolkit. This is a list of activities at your fingertips that you can turn to whenever you need a lift. I keep this list in my journal and on my phone for easy reference. It's best to write out your toolkit when you are feeling relaxed and inspired. Don't wait for life to throw you a curveball to think about self-care; that's when it is hardest to be creative and resourceful.

Self-care works best when it is kept fresh, evolving and responsive to the changing demands of everyday life, so generate lots of different options and choose different things from your Self-Care Toolkit to keep it effective. In Positive Psychology there is a term to describe this effect: it's called 'hedonic adaptation'[2]. Just as the results for your physical body reach a plateau if you don't keep your exercise routine changing, the benefits to our well-being also plateau if there isn't sufficient variety to your self-care. Remember to add new activities or take a look at a different pathway of the Vitality Wheel if you start feeling bored or fatigued, or your commitment to self-care wavers.

Don't wait for life to throw you a curveball to think about self-care; that's when it is hardest to be creative and resourceful.

THE SEVEN SECRETS OF SELF-CARE

1

Repeat after me:
'self-care isn't selfish',
keep repeating until you
believe it.

2

Give yourself permission
to take time out for you.

3

Make an appointment with
yourself and don't quibble about
it. It's important. Don't wait for a
good moment – they rarely come,
and bitterness about it at 9pm on
Sunday isn't good for anyone.

the self-care vitality wheel

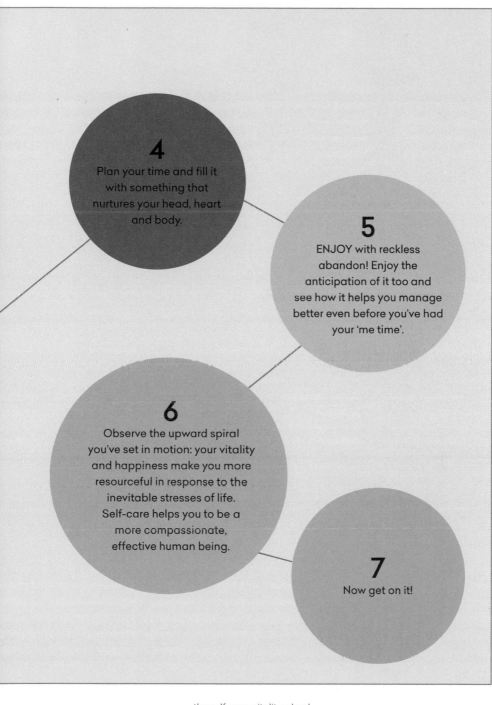

4

Plan your time and fill it with something that nurtures your head, heart and body.

5

ENJOY with reckless abandon! Enjoy the anticipation of it too and see how it helps you manage better even before you've had your 'me time'.

6

Observe the upward spiral you've set in motion: your vitality and happiness make you more resourceful in response to the inevitable stresses of life. Self-care helps you to be a more compassionate, effective human being.

7

Now get on it!

HOW TO MAKE SELF-CARE HAPPEN

▸ **Refer to your Self-Care Toolkit** or annotated Vitality Wheel in times of stress or whenever you need a boost of energy, calm or confidence. Pick an activity and feel how it helps you cope better in this moment.

▸ **Plan your down time.** Look for windows of opportunity in your week and make an appointment with yourself, then use the Vitality Wheel to help you make a loose plan of what you might do with that time. 'Me time' is precious, so don't fritter it away. The added benefit of planning your down time is that the anticipation of that activity doubles the joy and amplifies the positive impact on your well-being.

▸ **Use the Vitality Wheel** to make the most of precious 'spare moments'. How often do you find yourself with a spare half an hour and it feels so foreign that you don't know what to do with it? Use the Vitality Wheel to inspire you in that moment.

BEGINNING YOUR 'VITALITY JOURNAL'

▶ Even when you know that the commitment to self-care is important, it can be hard to make it happen. Why is this? Because carving any new habit is challenging. Also, the healthy and life-giving option is not always the easiest or most alluring, and our willpower simply isn't strong enough. As a yoga teacher, I know full well the benefits of yoga. I enjoy yoga and I have an infinite number of comforting sequences at my fingertips, but still the lure of the sofa can feel overwhelmingly tempting... I too am human. The tool that helps me make the commitment to self-care is journaling. I use my Vitality Journal to make self-care happen.

Your Vitality Journal is a record of all your well-being goals, activities and reflections. This process of journaling can create a feeling of ownership over your well-being, it gives direction and fine tunes your focus and commitment to self-care. Recording your actions enhances your feeling of accountability and helps you progress towards your goals.

Your Vitality Journal will help you get to know yourself better and is a self-care activity in itself. Choose a journal that really appeals to you, something that you're excited to write in. Record in it your name and state that you are making the commitment to your well-being. Write down your goals, brainstorm your Self-Care Toolkit and note down any 'aha' moments.

Include any actions you have taken to boost your happiness and well-being, whatever information you feel is relevant. Depending on your goals, this could be your intake of food, alcohol, exercise, sleep and rest, energy levels and mood. Write about how you feel after you've nourished yourself with self-care activities so you can see what is working for you. Use your journal to connect the dots between choices and outcomes.

Write in your Vitality Journal anything that inspires you, stick in clippings, quotes or images. Write about happy events you might like to remember. As a general rule, try not to use your journal to vent. It is far better to write down the toxic stuff on a piece of paper and then relish throwing it away. Reading negativity often leads to you re-experiencing those same emotions. Let your Vitality Journal be a wellspring of positivity so that if you have a spare minute to yourself you can 'fill your cup' just by flicking through it.

If right now the idea of journaling seems too much effort or it just simply doesn't resonate, that's OK, there are other options. You can keep notes on your phone or online calendar, or consider setting up a private Instagram account where you can record your happy moments. Just choose a strategy that feels do-able for you right now.

WILLPOWER, HABITS & LIFESTYLE CHANGES THAT STICK

▸ Generally speaking, we all know what we need to do to feel healthy, but making it happen and then keeping it going is another story entirely. In my own experience and from what I have observed with hundreds of clients, the most effective way to make change is in small, incremental steps. Elaborate, sweeping changes might yield splendid results, but it's exceedingly hard to sustain and when we fall off the wagon it can really knock our motivation. When you are integrating change inspired by the Vitality Wheel choose one activity or behaviour you want to develop and work on it until it is part of daily life. Once you have formed this new habit, then it's time to consider the next wave of change. With practice, you will find it gets easier to make changes that stick.

1. ACKNOWLEDGE THAT WILLPOWER ON ITS OWN IS NOT ENOUGH

Willpower isn't just limited to resisting unhealthy treats. We draw on our willpower to be polite, to mask irritation, to say the right thing, anything from being courteous on the road to being stuck on the phone to the call centre. Modern life is full of noise, stimulation, temptation and choice – the part of the brain responsible for willpower simply isn't powerful enough to help us make the right call every time. You'll have heard of the saying that willpower is a muscle that is strengthened each time you use it? I disagree. By the end of the day, when I am pooped, I am not empowered by the number of times I have called on my willpower, I am willpower fatigued. Habit is strengthened by repetition, whereas willpower is drained by constant use.

How can we overcome this willpower depletion? I think it is threefold. Firstly, reduce the number of decisions you have to make in a day by getting organized. We'll look more closely at how to do this in the chapter on Movement & Nutrition (see pages 80–97) in the form of primer statements. Secondly, dial down the volume of temptation by connecting with your values, which we explore in depth in the chapter on Values & Purpose (see pages 192–207). And finally, replenish your willpower reserves with soothing activities like rest, relaxation, working with your breath, being in nature, avoiding alcohol and minimizing over-stimulation with screens and gadgets. Good sleep is also essential for clear thinking and effective decision making.

2. KNOW YOUR 'WHY'

It's not enough to know what you want, you have to know why you want it. Articulating the purpose behind a lifestyle change is the thing that truly motivates you and helps you make the choices to achieve that change. Many people come to me saying they want to get fit. On its own that goal is insufficient to galvanize you when you are being tempted by life. You have to get clear on your 'why'. Your purpose is deeply personal and individual to you – some people set out to improve their fitness because they want to be a role model of healthy behaviour for their kids. Someone else's 'why' might be to reduce genetic risks of illness, while another person might be motivated by taking an adventure holiday. It's connecting with the deeper purpose that helps diminish temptation, keeping you on the path to where you want to be.

3. KNOW YOURSELF

You can't change anything until you are fully aware of your current behaviour and its consequences. Bring the behaviour you want to change to life by taking stock and noticing the choices you are currently making. Take an inventory in your Vitality Journal over a week: what happened, how did you respond and what was the outcome? Are your current strategies working? How can you do things differently? Readiness for change and acceptance that change is necessary are essential ingredients. If you're not ready, I would suggest revisiting your 'why' and making sure this is something you really care about.

4. BRAINSTORM YOUR REQUIRED ACTION

Once you've settled on a specific behaviour, you need to plan how you're going to do it. It helps to form a goal around it. So for example, if you want to boost your fitness you might choose to increase the amount of movement in your day. Start by giving yourself a realistic target of what you can commit to every day. Ten minutes is a reasonable daily time commitment and it is enough to create tangible changes to your health. Here's the trick – every day you do your ten minutes, pop a tick on your diary or calendar. When you have a run of ticks you won't want to break it and it's a really powerful visual tool. If you're motivated by writing a 'to-do' list, make sure you write your ten minutes of self-care at the top and remember that it's a non-negotiable.

5. WHAT'S NEXT?

Soon enough this new behaviour becomes habit and we transform our lives by making one healthy habit after another. Celebrate your accomplishments and consider what you can refine next. Keep taking small, steady steps towards your best self!

HOW YOGA CAN HELP

▸ Yoga has been a significant part of my life for over 20 years now. It was the thing that put me back together following my burnout. It's the activity I now turn to when I need to rest, and equally when I need to stand tall and connect with my personal power. While the presence of my yoga ritual has been constant, its form has varied widely, depending on life's circumstances and my needs at the time. This is a great strength, but it can also make yoga feel like a bit of a mine field. With so many 'styles' out there it can be really challenging to know where to begin. What I will say with great confidence, is that there is a type of yoga for everybody, and the yoga in this book is a great place to start even if you've never tried it before. Similarly, the sequences in this book can be a way of deepening your practice if you are experienced, because the simplicity might just allow you some different insights.

▸ Whether clients have come to me as a personal trainer, yoga teacher or psychologist, they have just about all been 'prescribed' yoga of some kind. I have used yoga to help people achieve better fitness, energy, confidence and a more positive relationship with their body. There are many clinical trials supporting what I've seen first-hand in my consulting room, with evidence suggesting that yoga is an effective method to help people with a range of conditions including anxiety[3], depression[4], schizophrenia[5], stress[6], post-traumatic stress disorder[7], hypertension[8], cardiovascular disease[9], multiple sclerosis[10], cancer[11], arthritis[12], diabetes[13], sleep issues[14], obesity[15] and osteoporosis[16] . I have done yoga with newborns, toddlers, teens, adults and a few beautiful souls in their nineties. There is without doubt, yoga appropriate for everybody.

The yoga in this book is a great place to start even if you've never tried it before.

YOGA & THE VITALITY WHEEL

▸ I teach from the 'viniyoga' lineage, where the
sequence is crafted around a specific goal. The yoga
in each chapter is designed to support each spoke of
the Vitality Wheel, giving you an opportunity to use
your body to support the tips and ideas. The yoga
in the Sleep, Rest, Relaxation and Breathing chapter
(see pages 78–79) is about calming, soothing and
quietening, as opposed to the yoga in the Goal-
setting chapter (see pages 190–191) which is about
creating a feeling of resolve and strength. I have also
included some affirmations which, coupled with
movement and your breathing, can feel very powerful.
If you're in any doubt, start with the yoga from the
chapters on Sleep and Relaxation (see pages 78–79)
or Coping Skills (see pages 124–125).

GUIDELINES ON PRACTISING YOGA

Practise at least one pose every single day, even
if it is just one pose while the kettle boils.

You don't need to be bendy to do this yoga – you do it
to become more bendy physically and more mentally
malleable to life in all its glory.

Yoga is not a performance sport – it is a tonic,
a deep form of nourishment. Give the sequences
in this book a go with an open mind and the intention
to lovingly tend to your mind and body.

Please move slowly and mindfully. Nothing should be painful
– challenging at times, yes, but never painful. Always use
your breath as your guide, breathing in and out through the
nose as naturally as possible. If you can breathe comfortably
in a yoga pose it should be safe. If there is any holding or
shortening of your breath, then please back off.

If you have any doubts, consult your doctor and seek out a
teacher who can guide you in person.

little gems ▸

▸ The Vitality Wheel
is designed to remind you
of the eight different ways you can
nourish yourself. The Vitality Wheel
spokes are: sleep, rest, relaxation and
breathing; movement and nutrition;
coping skills; physical environment; social
connection; mood boosters;
goal-setting and accomplishment;
and values and purpose.

▸ Work with as
many of the spokes as you
wish and skip straight to the
chapters that call to you.
The book doesn't need to be
read in chronological order
nor do you need to
work with all of the
Vitality Wheel.

▸ Make a mind map by
annotating a copy of the
Vitality Wheel, jotting down
the tools and tips that resonate
for you on each segment. Hang
it somewhere you will see it
regularly and turn to it when
you need help.

▶ Design your own Self-Care Toolkit by writing down the resources and activities you can turn to when you need it the most. Use your toolkit when you feel stressed, to plan your down time and to make the most of precious spare time.

▶ To help you build healthy habits, start a Vitality Journal. Choose something you feel excited to write in and record any information relevant to your well-being goals and anything that fills you with joy.

▶ Sustainable change is best achieved in small steps. Focus on one behaviour or one habit at a time. Recognize that willpower on its own is not enough. Overcome willpower depletion by getting organized. Get clear on why you want to create this change and remind yourself of your purpose to keep you on track. Tick off every day you take that action until it becomes habit and you are ready to integrate a new change.

notes to myself ›

Remember to add new activities or take a look at a different pathway of the Vitality Wheel if you start feeling bored or fatigued, or your commitment to self-care wavers.

one

SLEEP, REST, RELAXATION & BREATHING

▸ When my kids were tiny, I never felt I slept deeply because I found it so hard to detach myself and switch off. The relationship between quality of sleep and quality of mind was never more apparent to me, and my mantra quickly became 'sleep for sanity'. Following disturbed nights, I would feel low and quick to anger for days. Even now, after months of fairly decent sleep, just one interrupted night's sleep still has a marked impact on my mood and focus. If you're feeling this way too, it's only natural. You will return to a more abundant you when the possibility of sleep also returns, and until then, you can learn to use self-care techniques to prop yourself up.

THE IMPORTANCE OF SLEEP

▸ I think sleep tends to get a pretty bad rap these days. Attitudes like 'I'll sleep when I'm dead' and 'FOMO' reflect a cultural norm of seeing sleep deprivation as essential to success. Let's be clear, sleep is a fundamental human need. There is nothing lazy, selfish or indulgent about giving yourself the chance of decent sleep. When life gets full to the brim it is often the first thing that is sacrificed and this is precisely when we need it the most! We need sleep for cellular renewal, for the health of our nervous system and immune system, to regulate our body weight, for our mood, for consolidation of memory and for our cognitive performance. Lack of sleep is connected with the increased risk of heart attack, stroke, diabetes, obesity, stress and inflammation of body tissue. It also leads to a loss of brain cells and it speeds up signs of ageing.

If you are in the midst of a crisis or recovering from a period of acute stress, the best place to start your healing journey is with sleep, rest and relaxation. Obvious, right? But ask any parent, carer, student, high-level exec or business owner and they are likely to laugh at this. The reality is that even if that's what you desperately need and want, you can't always get it. With 27 per cent of Britons experiencing poor quality sleep on a regular basis and more than one-third getting only five to six hours of sleep per night[17], if you too find yourself in a state of chronic sleep deficit, you're not alone. You might not be able to get decent sleep, there may be little time to rest, but there is a way to relax and restore your body's energy that comes close: breathing.

During and after times of upheaval, our bodies are flooded with stress hormones that can leave us feeling depleted, anxious and depressed. The sympathetic nervous system has been sent into overdrive and that chronic experience of 'fight or flight' can make you feel like you've been hit by a truck. We need to stimulate the parasympathetic nervous system (PNS) – the part that is responsible for the 'rest and digest' functions of the body – to mediate the effects of these stress hormones. The best way to promote the PNS is by getting adequate sleep, making time for rest and relaxation and by returning to a more natural, relaxed and expansive way of breathing.

If you need more motivation to get decent sleep back on the radar, the facts and figures around quality of sleep and performance are pretty startling. In as little as two weeks of getting six hours of sleep per night, performance decline is similar to going a whole 24 hours without sleeping. For people getting just four hours a night, the drop off is the same as going 48 hours without sleep[18] . Being awake for 17 hours can result in the same level of cognitive impairment as having a blood alcohol level of .05 per cent. Add just another few hours of awake time and we go up to the equivalent of 0.1 per cent, which is legally drunk[19]. 'You snooze, you lose' is clearly a dangerous attitude to hold. Making the commitment to giving yourself the best possible chance of adequate sleep is anything but indulgent – it's essential.

PROMOTING BETTER SLEEP

▸ There is no magic bullet to guarantee a good night's sleep. There isn't one solution for all and while there are broad principles, some experimentation is required to see what works for you.

What is a good night's sleep?

▸ Good sleep doesn't need to be in one unbroken stretch. Throughout most of human history (until the advent of artificial light) sleep was divided into two separate periods, rather than the revered uninterrupted stretch to which we now aspire, so segmented sleep is very normal. The period of wakefulness that might last a few hours was historically used for self-reflection, prayer, meditation, reading, writing and sex. The wakefulness some experience now might just be a natural expression of pre-industrial sleeping patterns.

What puts us to sleep?

▸ There are two main ways that your body puts you to sleep, and knowing these mechanisms helps you make choices more conducive to better sleep. Sleeping and waking cycles are guided by the circadian rhythm – your master clock – which is individual to you. Long-haul travel interrupts this, as does the blue light emitted from screens, which suppresses melatonin production. Getting plenty of natural light in the morning can combat the effects of being in front of a screen during the working day.

The other mechanism is sleep pressure, which builds up as you stay awake and releases when you go to bed. This explains why falling asleep on the sofa at 9pm can scupper your sleep when you finally make it to bed. Well-timed naps, on the other hand, can promote better sleep at night.

Are you getting enough sleep?

▸ Surviving on too little sleep is not a badge of honour: most adults need seven to nine hours. You may get by on less, but for how long and at what cost? Sleep needs are individual, so get to know how many hours you personally need to function well and make sleep a genuine priority. If you find yourself madly rushing about trying to get things done at night at the expense of time in bed, ask yourself: 'Does this really need to be done right now?' Zoning out in front of the TV is not as relaxing as getting the sleep you need.

Be mindful of stimulation

▸ One of the major causes of insomnia is the inability to relax, so pay attention to your levels of tension and arousal through the whole day, not just at night. Reduce your intake of caffeine and sugar and I avoid coffee after 2pm. Even if you think caffeine has no effect on your sleep, it may still be affecting your adrenals. This applies to your visual diet as well. We can be very stimulated by what we choose to read, watch and listen to throughout our day. If you are having a tough time sleeping, leave the thrilling stuff for another time and opt for books, films and music that soothe and calm you.

Eliminate as much light as possible. Lower the wattage of your bedroom light bulb or use the hall light instead. Switch off your electronic devices and don't check them if you wake. Black-out blinds can be life changing, or wear an eye mask.

Keep it cool. The ideal bedroom temperature is around 18 degrees Celcius.

Make your bedroom a haven. Use linen that you can't wait to slide into, décor that you find soothing and a clean and clutter-free environment.

CREATING YOUR PRE-BEDTIME RITUAL

Keep it consistent. Aim for the same bedtime and rise time each day. While many sleep experts advocate getting to bed by around 10pm, we need to take into consideration our own body clock and daily commitments. See what works best with the demands of your current circumstances and experiment with the windows of time that help you best drift off and wake feeling refreshed.

Digital detox. Aim for at least 30 minutes of screen-free time before bed. The negative effects of electronics on sleep quality are well known, but most adults use some kind of gadget in the hour before bed. If you think that your eReader helps you unwind, think again! The light emitted causes the same kind of reduction in sleepiness and disruption to your circadian rhythms as other electronics[20]. Read a printed book, listen to music or an audio book as an alternative.

Relax your body. Take a bath or shower or try some calming breath work or gentle yoga (see pages 78–79).

Relax your mind. If it is swirling with thoughts, try a 'brain dump' and write down any nagging thoughts using a pen and paper. Ask yourself whether these things are as pressing as you first thought. Write down anything you genuinely need to tackle tomorrow so you can let it slip from your mind. If there are pressing issues that regularly interfere with your ability to relax, reach out and talk to someone.

End the day on a positive note. Get out your Vitality Journal and complete the exercise Martin Seligman calls 'The Three Blessings'[21]. Write down three positive things that happened in your day and importantly, why they happened. There is no right or wrong here, whatever comes to mind. Notice how this changes the quality of your mood and helps focus your mind on more constructive thoughts.

Prime yourself for sleep. Cue your mind by wearing pyjamas that you love and using soothing scents such as lavender on your body or your pillow.

TIPS TO HELP YOU GET TO SLEEP

▸ Often it's our thinking that gets in the way of decent shut-eye. Rather than attempting to clear the mind, try anchoring it on thoughts that help you relax. I have a series of mantras that I rely on to help me get to sleep and get back to sleep when I am woken.

▸ As you lie down to sleep, give yourself permission to rest. Use the mantra: 'It is just time for me to rest'. If something else pops up, tell yourself it's not time for that now, or jot it down and let it go. Or use the mantra: 'There is nothing required of me right now'. It helps you relish the absence of effort and sink into rest even if sleep seems elusive.

▸ If you still feel it's hard to unwind or you are finding it difficult to get back to sleep, try the following mantra: 'If I can't sleep, I will rest. If I can't slow my mind, I will soften my body. I receive the inhalation, I surrender to the exhalation. I become my breath'. As you repeat it, work on physically softening any tension you find in your body and feeling the sensations of your breathing.

▸ Don't count the hours of sleep you have or haven't had. Tell yourself that you had as much sleep as you got and you will use self-care to compensate for any shortfall of sleep.

REST AND RELAXATION

▸ Even when you are getting adequate sleep, the opportunity to stop, rest and relax is a vital part of caring for your health and well being. We live in a caffeinated, adrenaline-fuelled world, with competing demands placed upon us. For many people, there is little opportunity to top up our depleted energy bank. As a general rule, the importance of quality R&R is vastly underrated and often stigmatized as laziness – this is simply not true. Every human needs a time where they can just 'be', by which I mean time where there is an absence of striving, effort or problem solving, a complete absence of ambition.

People regularly say to me that they just don't have time to rest... but without it, soon enough your system will falter like mine, and it's more that you can't afford not to take the time out to rest. If you leave yourself open to fatigue, you become susceptible to burnout, anxiety, depression, illness and injury. Chances are the enforced rest will come at a time of even less convenience.

- **Time out** allows healing, cleansing and purification to occur, from physiological regeneration on a cellular level to a replenishment of the energy stores on an emotional and psychological level. We often associate the benefits of activities such as yoga with stress management, but it's shown to have tangible positive effects on the immune system as well[22]. The gentle yoga practice included on pages 78–79 is a perfect place to begin a short daily ritual.

- **Seeking stillness** stimulates growth and cultivates sensitivity. We all need time to regroup and to take stock. This quiet reflection helps us to think clearly and make sound decisions that are more in tune with our goals.

- **Time spent on your own** in contemplation opens your eyes to opportunities. It changes your focus so that you can go back to your daily routine with fresh perspective. We now know from MRI scans that mindfulness-based meditation significantly changes the structure of the brain involved in the modulation of arousal and mood in just eight weeks[23]. For the first time in medical history the effect of meditation on well-being was shown as a change in the brain's grey matter.

- **Rest** puts you back in touch with your body so you know when to push and when to yield – vital in establishing a healthy balance.

- **We are so used to being busy** that we forget how to slow down. I think we can even get addicted to busyness because when we pause, we are confronted with the bubbling up of thoughts, sensations, feelings and memories. Sometimes this can be unsettling, so if stillness doesn't resonate right now, that's OK, there are many different ways of relaxing.

● ● ● ● ● ● ● ●

MY FAVOURITE WAYS TO UNWIND

RESTORATIVE YOGA

▸ This is also known as lying down on your mat and not moving, maybe even sleeping... honestly, lying on my mat and allowing myself to drop off was the greatest tonic for me. It was a great alternative to going to bed because it avoided the great pressure to sleep. If I chose a restorative yoga pose with the intention to relax rather than sleep, I could be in that pose for five minutes and feel I had the benefit. If I 'dipped under' and had a snooze there, bonus.

Technically speaking, restorative yoga poses are particular shapes that you hold with support like cushions and blankets, most often done lying down. Rather than fall asleep, the intention is to keep your mind anchored either on the physical sensations of your body relaxing or on your breathing. If you are exhausted or suffering from a sleep deficit, don't fight the urge to fall asleep in these poses. It's what your body needs and if you are safe and comfortable, why not? Restorative yoga poses aren't just for people who are feeling fatigued, they are a great way to re-energize, even when you are in tip-top shape. These yoga poses can stimulate blood flow to areas in the body that have become 'stuck' and open up the breathing passageways to allow deep revitalisation.

EASY MEDITATIONS

▶ If the thought of meditation turns you off, hang in there. Some meditation techniques can make you feel agitated – it's a matter of working with a meditative tool that fits you. If you're feeling overstimulated, trying to clear your mind in a seated meditation practice can be hard. What may work better is to tether your mind to a mantra or sensation:

- **Take a meditative shower.** Be present and let the water unwind you. Immerse yourself in the sensation of the water against your skin, connect with the cleansing properties of it, feeling your troubles wash away with the water.

- **Feel the breath with yoga mudras (hand gestures).** Sit tall in a comfortable position either on a bolster on the floor or in a chair. Relax your shoulders and jaw and allow the back of your hands to rest on your thighs. Take a few relaxed breaths – noticing how it feels to be breathing. Gently touch your thumb to your first fingertip. Notice how this directs your breath into your abdomen and feel how soothing this is. Breathe for ten breaths or a few minutes. The second mudra is to curl the remaining three fingers gently in towards the palm. Feel how this moves the breath into your chest and imagine your heart opening. Then draw your thumbs into the centre of your palms and wrap the fingers around them gently. Feel how this now directs the breath into the collar bones and upper back, melting tension and giving an uplifting quality. Keeping the hands as they are, move into the fourth mudra by bringing the backs of the fingers and knuckles to touch, your inner wrists facing upwards in front of your body around navel height. This integrates the breath in all three areas – feel how expansive and relaxed your breathing has become. Then release your hands back to your thighs and enjoy a few more breaths here before re-entering your day.

- **'I am' meditations.** You can make this a formal sitting practice or repeat these while on your commute, at your desk or the kitchen sink. As you breathe in repeat the words 'I am' and as you breathe out you choose a word that cultivates how you want to feel. I often use words such as: OK, calm, energetic, resourceful, strong, patient, loving, loved, resolute, healthy and blessed. You can keep repeating the one phrase or change with each exhalation. If you prefer, just stick with 'I' on the inhalation and 'am' on the exhalation – that fact is irrefutable.

- **Seek out beauty.** Wherever you are, be on the lookout for something inspiring and uplifting. Beauty lifts your spirits and opens you up to an experience of awe. From your desk at work, maybe it's the cloudscape. Perhaps it's the trees you can focus on during your commute to work or the school run. Keep a vase of flowers at home to gaze upon. Be aware of artwork around you and notice architectural beauty too.

- **Create a relaxation library.** This can include magazines, books, photo albums, CDs, TV programmes, films – even your Vitality Journal counts, especially if you use it to gather happy memories. Build a collection of mindfulness or meditation resources and use these to be led into a calm state.

- **Practise yoga nidra.** This is a type of guided relaxation, which is not only a great way to unwind but research has shown that it can also help alleviate depression and anxiety[24]. Find a comfy spot and snuggle in.

Beauty lifts your spirits
and opens you up to
an experience of awe.

Sit upright and soften any physical tension. We tend to tighten our forehead, eyes, jaw, neck, shoulders, hands and abdomen. Repeat the mantras 'I release what I no longer need' or 'I let go of what no longer serves me'.

Take some gentle head turns, gazing right and then left to oil the neck.

Stretch the side of your neck by taking your right ear towards you right shoulder and then your left ear towards your left shoulder. Repeat this a few times on each side.

Drop your chin towards your chest and feel the back of the neck release. Take your chin over towards your right shoulder, back to the sternum and over to the left. Repeat a few times on each side, allowing your head to be heavy and your face to soften.

Roll your shoulders. As you breathe in, lift your shoulders up; as you breathe out, roll them back and down.

Circle your wrists and ankles in both directions.

Sitting tall, take a twist by bringing your hands to your right thigh and looking over your right shoulder. Repeat the twist to the left.

Feel your breath. Rest your hands on the back of your thighs with the palms facing upwards. You can do this under your desk without anyone seeing. As you inhale, open your hands wide and feel how this opens up your whole body to receive a more expansive breath in. As you breathe out, make a gentle fist, feeling how this helps you empty your lungs more effectively.

Enjoy some beautiful scent. Hand creams, pulse point roll-on scents or facial mists with incredible scents can calm, soothe or energize.

Add a drop of edible flower remedy to your water and as you drink it affirm the quality of the flower. In this way I literally feel like I am drinking a cup of 'courage' or 'calm'.

Earth your brow by resting your forehead on something solid. Think of Homer Simpson saying 'Doh!' and bringing his hand to his forehead. The body is hard-wired to do this in times of stress because it soothes the nervous system. Fold your hands on your desk and rest your forehead on the back of your hands – this is instantly calming. Or make two fists and gently press the base of your thumb into your forehead.

TOPPING UP YOUR ENERGY BANK
WITH YOUR BREATHING

▶ When sleep, and even rest and relaxation, seem hard to access, remember you always have your breathing to work with. There is a strong connection between the quality of your breathing, your health and the quality of your mind. Just as stress affects the way we breathe, the way we breathe can affect our psychophysiology, so learning how to breathe freely is fundamental to healing[25]. The yoga sequences at the end of this chapter are designed to help re-pattern your breathing, helping establish a more natural, balanced and relaxed rhythm.

Recent research by psychologist and happiness expert Emma Seppälä supports these ideas from the yoga tradition. Seppälä and her team worked with veterans recently returned from Iraq and Afghanistan with trauma[26].Teaching them a breathing-based meditation practice designed to calm the nervous system was found to reduce anxiety and symptoms of post-traumatic stress disorder. The really encouraging thing is that these positive effects held even a year after the intervention, suggesting that breathing techniques can have a lasting, if not permanent impact. A favourite mantra of mine is 'spacious breath: spacious mind'. Your breath is the one thing you are doing all the time anyway, so learn to work with its healing power. Here's a way to start:

- Find a comfortable position for your body and connect with your breathing – don't do anything to change your breathing and don't try to breathe a certain way. Don't think about your breath, just feel the sensations of your breath. Notice the inhalation, the pause after you breathe in, the exhalation and the pause after you breathe out. Allow those natural pauses to be there without any effort to lengthen them, unless that feels good to you.

- Observe where in your body you feel the breath moving to. You may feel it in your chest, up into your collar bones, around your shoulder blades, through your sides, your abdomen and even your lower back. Just observe and watch the flow of the breath.

- Observe the expansive quality of the in breath and the gentle dropping back to your centre with the out breath. Feel the fresh energy brought in with your inhalation and that sense of letting go with the exhalation.

Do this exercise at any time in your day and your breath will tend to smooth itself out without any will or conscious intervention. In my experience it is impossible to feel stressed when you are breathing well and you can do this anywhere, anytime!

little gems ▸

▸ There is no badge of honour in denying yourself the chance to sleep, rest and relax. There is nothing lazy, selfish or indulgent about it. It is essential for your physical, mental and emotional health.

▸ Make sure you are getting enough sleep, especially when you are ill, stressed or burdened. Most adults need seven to nine hours.

▸ Developing your ability to relax will help you sleep. Factor in micro moments of relaxation throughout your day with gentle movement, breath work and mantras.

▸ Give yourself time and space to relax and renew with restorative yoga, easy meditations, appreciating beauty and building your own relaxation library.

▸ Reduce your levels of stimulation throughout your day, monitoring your intake of caffeine, sugar, alcohol and screens.

sleep, rest, relaxation & breathing

▶ Develop your own pre-bedtime ritual with ways to relax your mind with a 'brain dump' or the 'three blessings' exercise, relax your body with a shower, bath or gentle stretching. Keep your sleeping patterns consistent and commit to a 30-minute digital detox.

▶ Create the ideal environment for sleep by minimizing light, keeping it cool and making your bedroom a haven for relaxation.

▶ If you can't sleep, don't worry, just rest. If you don't have time to stop (make time!) just be with your breathing. Sleep, rest and relaxed breathing all heal the nervous system and mediate stress hormones.

▶ Use your mantras: Sleep for sanity. Does this REALLY need to be done right now? It is just time for me to rest. There is nothing required of me right now. If I can't sleep, then I will rest. If I can't slow my mind, I will soften my body. I receive the inhalation, I surrender to the exhalation. I release what I no longer need. I let go of what no longer serves me. Spacious breath: spacious mind.

▶ Work with your breath by simply feeling the sensations of it. Nothing fancy required, just notice the inhalation, a tiny pause, the exhalation and another pause.

YOGA TO HELP YOU REST, RELAX & SLEEP

These restorative yoga poses are held in stillness while breathing calmly.

Child's pose

Begin on all fours with your knees at least hip-width apart. Breathe out and sink your bottom to your heels and bring your forehead down onto the floor or your folded hands, softening your shoulders. Or bring your arms, one at a time, around behind you so your palms face upwards beside your feet. Be guided by the comfort of your neck, shoulders and upper back. Stay here for 5–10 relaxed breaths, longer if it feels good. Feel how breathing into this shape melts tension in the back of your body.

Pigeon

From all fours, bring your right knee to your right hand, bring your right foot in front of your left hip, slide your left leg further back behind you and lower your body down towards the floor. Bring your forehead to rest on the floor or on the back of your hands. Keep your elbows wide apart and soften your shoulders. Consciously soften the muscles of your back, buttocks and thighs. Hold for 5–15 breaths, focusing on lengthening your out breath, then repeat on the other side.

Legs over the sofa or up the wall

Have a cushion and blanket within easy reach.
Sit on the floor with your side towards either the
base of a wall or the sofa. Carefully lie on your
back and swing your legs up the wall or onto the
sofa. The wall provides a more restorative effect,
but can be a strong hamstring stretch – be guided
by your comfort. Place the cushion beneath your
head, drape a blanket over you. Stay here for five
minutes or more and allow your body to be held.
There is nothing to be done but soften and release.

Savasana

Gather a folded blanket to place under your head,
a bolster or rolled blanket to place beneath your
knees, an eye pillow if you have one and if the
temperature requires, a blanket to drape over
you. Lie on your back with your head and knees
supported by the props. Have your feet at least hip-
width apart and let your toes drop out to the sides.
Place your arms 45 degrees away from your body
with your palms facing upwards, allowing your
fingertips to curl in towards your palms. Feel your
body melt into the floor and the support beneath
you. Say to yourself: 'There is nothing required
of me right now' and tether your attention to the
sensations of your breathing and your body as it
relaxes. Be here for at least five minutes.

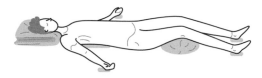

two

MOVEMENT & NUTRITION

▸ I vividly remember my mum cajoling me to eat dinner after Charlotte was born. I couldn't be bothered. I was just desperate to get my head down while she was asleep, but she reminded me of my dad's words: 'If you eat like a sparrow you get a bird's brain'. As a psychiatrist he was well versed in how to achieve mental clarity. If you want to think straight you've got to eat. Second time round with Ted I made sure the house was stocked with crumpets, baked beans and anything simple (I won't mention the entire rainbow cake that I devoured in the first week of his life) that I could shovel in and keep myself well-nourished to avoid a repeat experience of energetic bankruptcy.

If you're in the midst of a crisis or recovering from burnout this is not the time to be embarking on a spartan eating regime or rigorous exercise, but still this chapter is important for you. We need to feed the brain and nourish our mood with movement and nutrition to best help us cope with the challenges we face. When it comes to exercise, you need to heal your system from the ravages of stress before you return to really exerting yourself. If you are feeling depleted, then head to the chapter sleep and relaxation (see page 56) because the yoga there will sooth and uplift you without further taxing your energy stores (see pages 78–79). If you want to create change to your physical body, or are looking for greater zest and resilience, then this chapter will give you the tools to make those sustainable healthy lifestyle choices happen and the yoga will support these goals too.

When I reflect on my journey back to wellness, it's no surprise that my return to a focus on work and working out coincided with Charlotte starting nursery... there was time, space and energy for something else! It felt like we had weathered the storm and I was 'coming back'. As my energy stores began to build I could sense that it was time to take a look at my physical shape... I embarked on what I called my 'eight weeks to a better body–mind challenge'. This was all about getting healthy eating and more vigorous exercise back on the radar in a sustainable way. The goal shaping this period of my life was to get in the best possible physical shape for trying for another baby.

The topics of exercise and nutrition are rich and plentiful grounds for exploration but for our self-care purposes I want to keep it simple, real and achievable. At the heart of my message here is the recognition that relying on willpower alone is not enough. Welcome to being human, you can stop giving yourself a hard time. The way we make up for willpower deficit is by using strategies to reduce the number of decisions we have to make and secondly, using psychological tools to dial down the volume on temptation so our willpower is not so taxed.

So, rather than a one-size-fits-all approach, we're going to take a look at the psychology of healthy exercise and eating. I'll give you broad principles and tips that you can use as inspiration for brainstorming your self-care activities around exercise and nutrition.

A little reminder before we get underway about changes to your diet and exercise patterns: whatever changes you make, aim to make them long term. Take small, steady steps to eating and moving for a healthier, happier you. Grand, sweeping changes just aren't sustainable.

THE PRINCIPLES OF HEALTHY EXERCISE

1. Move daily for a minimum of twenty minutes

It's not about exercise; it's about movement. It can bedancing with your kids, gardening, vacuuming or just plain walking. Any movement counts.

2. Move for mental health

It's not just about rippling abs and toned thighs. Exercising will boost your clarity of thought and creativity, release your stress and help you to make better decisions. Remind yourself that this isn't an indulgence, it's an essential part of your self-care routine.

3. Keep it varied and keep it fun

Sustainable commitment to exercise is all about finding a way of moving that is intrinsically enjoyable to you. Please firmly cast aside the notion that exercise needs to hurt to be effective. Leave the 'no pain, no gain' mentality for elite athletes. In my experience, if I don't genuinely enjoy my training I am not going to persist at it, so be prepared to try different things. Challenging your body and mind in different ways will keep your motivation fresh and prevents your physical results from plateauing.

4. Plan ahead

Spot your windows of opportunity and get organized. Change doesn't happen on its own, you need to be prepared to do things differently. Research classes or sports you might like and at times that suit your lifestyle. Keep spare kit in your car so you never miss an opportunity. Get the kids or your friends involved and make it a priority in your everyday life. If all else fails, you have your yoga routine at the end of this chapter (see pages 96–97) to do at home – no excuses!

5. Work with what you've got

Even just five minutes is always better than nothing. It doesn't have to be done all at once. Movement has a cumulative effect, so keep investing the time where you can.

HOW TO MAKE EXERCISE HAPPEN

▸ You don't need a gym membership or fancy equipment, all you need is your body! Step outside and take a walk. Use the environment around you – hills, stairs and benches for step-ups, press-ups and dips. Learn some simple body weight exercises, such as squats and lunges, and intersperse them with walking or jogging intervals. Get out of the habit of considering only structured exercise as valuable. What is your incidental movement like? Can you stand instead of sit? Walk instead of drive?

Sometimes I swap my exercise routine for a zoo visit with my six-year-old... same amount of running around! Rather than meet for a sedentary coffee with a friend make your order to go and walk together?

Make a point to exercise early in your day. Just a short bout of exercise is good for commitment to healthy choices – after you exercise you are less likely to make poor food choices because you won't want to negate your earlier efforts.

Prime yourself to make healthy movement choices. Proactively think about the things that get in the way of you engaging in exercise and brainstorm solutions to overcome them. Use the form of 'If X happens... then I will do Y'[27]. These statements help you overcome the willpower deficit and will result in you making better decisions more often. So if you had a run planned, your primer statement could be: if it's raining, then I will roll out my yoga mat at home. Or when fatigue is a barrier to exercise: if I am tired, then I will get up and choose something gentle; I will still move because I know it will re-energize me. Or if time pressure is a barrier: if I can't get a minute to myself, then I will turn on some favourite tunes and bop away while cooking dinner.

For years I've been banging on about the value of 'incidental' exercise – all movement, not just organized exercise counts when it comes to health and fitness benefits. That means cleaning the bathroom can be just as effective as a gym workout and a recent study[28] shows us how to fine-tune the potency of everyday movement. And it all comes down to your mind set.

The study used 'housekeepers' who spend their entire working day engaged in the physical activity of cleaning hotel rooms. One group of housekeepers were informed of the benefits of exercise and given concrete information about the physical effects of their specific work tasks i.e. that just 15 minutes of vacuuming can burn 50 calories. They were told also that their typical workday far exceeds the national health guidelines for daily exercise.

The other group were given the same info about the benefits of exercise, but weren't informed that their work tasks actually constitute 'exercise'. Comparing the results between these two groups could determine whether there was any benefit to being aware of what serves as exercise.

The study tracked the progress of the housekeepers after one month. After just four weeks of knowing that their job constitutes exercise, the maids lost an average of two pounds, lowered their blood pressure by ten points and reduced their body fat, all without any change to their diet or additional exercise. This change was created just by being mindful of their movement and its positive effects! The comparison group stayed in the same shape they were in at the beginning of the study.

These results clearly demonstrate the power of the mind. So the next time you're labouring in the garden or opt to take the stairs, acknowledge that you are indeed honing your abs, firming the biceps or whittling down your thighs. As you move, look for ways that you can accelerate potential changes to your body just by harnessing the power of your mind!

THE PRINCIPLES OF HEALTHY EATING

▸ **The key to sustainable healthy eating is to make good choices most of the time.**
Eat unprocessed foods – fresh and whole. Fill up on protein (meat, fish and eggs), fresh fruit and veg, rather than carbs. Go easy on the junk food. There is never a good time to start, so just start living with this principle now. If you fall off the wagon, start again now, not tomorrow, not next week. Now.

▸ **Work with the 'energy in, energy out equation'.**
If you are trying to lose weight or reduce your body fat, you will need to burn more energy than you consume.

▸ **Respect your hunger.**
Get to know it again and really listen to it. Don't let yourself get starving-hungry or 'hangry' – this is when you are likely to make poor food choices. Stop eating when you're full. By eating slowly and mindfully you have a better chance of gauging when you are full. Acknowledge too when you are reaching for food for reasons other than hunger. Find other ways to fill that void or if you can't fight the urge, eat life-giving things, not junk that sabotages you.

▶ **Feed your brain and nourish your mood.**
Don't expect to feel energetic and think clearly if you haven't eaten enough. Don't expect to feel calm and relaxed if you are pumping your body full of caffeine and sugar. So feed your brain and nourish your mood by eating regular, life-giving meals.

▶ **Get organized and get prepared.**
Plan your meals and write out your shopping list. To minimize the number of food choices you have to make in your day write down what you plan to eat tomorrow and make sure those choices are available to you. Prepare it and take it with you if need be. You can even plan when you are going to indulge and how you can compensate for it later. Have healthy options at your fingertips – the easiest thing has to be healthy.

HOW TO MAKE HEALTHY EATING HAPPEN

KNOW YOURSELF & TAKE ACTION

▸ Become aware, accountable and take ownership of your nutrition. Keep a record of what you eat and drink in your Vitality Journal (see page 41). Use this information to really get to know yourself: your strengths and weaknesses. In terms of your nutrition, what are you doing well and what are the areas that need some attention? Have you mastered one meal of the day, but the others need some refinement? Are your meals pretty good, but could your snacks be improved? You know the kind of changes you need to make – start brainstorming your solutions and do something about it, one step at a time.

IDENTIFY YOUR SWAPS

▸ What are some of the things that you can (relatively painlessly) swap for something else? For example, for me coffee is a 'gateway'– I'm tempted to add sugar and then I want more sugary things such as cakes and biscuits. Green tea, on the other hand, has me reaching for healthier snack alternatives and keeps sugar cravings at bay. But that's just me. What can you substitute?

ARE YOU A MODERATOR OR AN ABSTAINER?

▶ You're a moderator if you can enjoy just the occasional indulgence and feel stressed at the thought of eliminating something from your diet. You're an abstainer if you have trouble stopping at just one and cope better when the temptation is removed altogether[29]. Be honest with yourself, decide if you are a moderator or an abstainer and plan your own healthy eating and shopping strategy accordingly. Maybe you can work with both principles – for example, I don't want to entertain the thought of life without burgers, red wine and chocolate, so that would make me a moderator. However, I'm also an abstainer because I admit to having trouble stopping at just one. If I have milk chocolate in the house, I can't stop at just one row, so to avoid that problem I abstain from having it in the house. I buy fancypants dark chocolate and eat just a little.

PRIME YOUR BRAIN

▶ Anticipate situations that make it hard to stick to healthy food choices and plan how to deal with it. Brainstorm your 'If... then' primer statements for healthy eating and write them down so you're not relying on willpower. So, for example, if I'm having a coffee, I'll make it with skimmed milk and no sugar. If a friend wants to catch up, then I'll suggest a walk rather than our connection revolving around food. If I'm out for dinner and I fancy a dessert, then I will share one.

SAVOUR YOUR INDULGENCE!

▸ The principle behind sustainable healthy eating
is to make good decisions most of the time. So my
favourite advice is, if you are going to indulge, then
savour it! There is more joy in a single savoured
chocolate than in a handful gobbled with guilt.
You might find you don't need to consume as much
to satisfy your desire and you possibly won't crave
it again for a while. If need be, plan how you can
accommodate for this indulgence so you can enjoy
it guilt free.

● ● ● ● ● ● ● ●

little gems ›

▸ Whether you're feeling full of beans or burnt out, eating and moving well is the cornerstone of your well-being. If you are at a low ebb, choose gentle and soothing movement, and eat to nourish your mood.

▸ Willpower is not enough on its own to sustain clean eating and regular exercise – use primer statements to help you overcome barriers and plan your week to reduce the number of decisions you face.

▸ Keep your movement varied and fun and know that it's not just about your body, it's about beating stress and boosting creativity too. Amplify the benefits by harnessing the power of your mind and noticing the effects of movement.

▸ Aim for change that you can keep up. Sweeping change might create impressive results, but if you can't sustain it, the results won't last either. Small, steady steps to new habits are the best.

▸ Move daily for a total of at least twenty minutes and remember any movement counts.

▸ Sustainable healthy eating is about making good choices most of the time and creating a balance between the energy you take in and the energy you expend. Listen to your hunger, identify your swaps and truly savour any indulgences.

notes to myself ▸

YOGA TO BOOST YOUR METABOLIC FIRE & FOR SHAPE & TONE

Plie mountain breath

Stand with your feet one and a half times shoulder-width apart and your toes facing out to 45 degrees and sink down into a squat. Inhale and straighten your legs and raise your arms out and up above your head. Exhale and bend your knees into a squat and lower your arms back down. Repeat six to ten times, feeling a sense of liveliness around your body.

Step-out lunges

Stand with your feet hip-width apart at the back of your yoga mat. Inhale and take a big step forwards with your right foot and bend your right knee deeply, taking your left knee down towards the floor without touching. Exhale and step the right foot back. Inhale and step your left foot out and lunge. Exhale and step the left foot back. Keep alternating with the step out lunge and repeat 5–10 times with each leg. Feel the heat of your internal fire.

Wide leg fold

Stand with your feet twice shoulder-width apart, with the outer edges of your feet parallel. Inhale and place your hands on your hips and lift your heart up. Exhale and soften your knees, hinge at your hips and bring your fingertips to the floor. Your knees can stay generously bent to focus on releasing your spine or you can work your legs straighter to stretch your hamstrings deeper – you choose whichever feels more replenishing. Take 5–10 breaths here to refresh.

Chi infinity slides

Stand with your feet one and a half times shoulder-width apart and your toes facing forwards. Inhale and bring your hands together at your heart. Exhale and turn your right toes to point out at 45 degrees, bend your right knee and slide your hands down and around in a circle forming one half of the infinity symbol. Inhale and turn your right toes back to facing forwards and slide your hands back to prayer pose at the heart. Exhale and turn your left toes out, bend your left knee and slide your hands in a circle to the left forming the other half of the infinity symbol. Inhale and turn your left toes back to facing forwards and bring your hands back to your heart. Repeat six times on each side again, feeling the energy this liberates.

three

COPING SKILLS

▶ This sounds laughable now but it was all the laundry that tipped me over the edge – everything required by a poor cherub with reflux, the bits my dad needed and while my mum was recuperating, her needs too. I was caught up thinking about the thousands of loads I had ahead of me. In reality I had to tackle two loads a day (as well as tending to a new-born and delivering daily supplies to my father) but in my head I was doing today's washing, tomorrow's washing and it all spooled out endlessly in front of me. A simple tool to chop things down was all it took to reign in that unhelpful thinking.

The Coping Skills pathway of the Vitality Wheel taps into the power of your mind and empowers you with concepts that will help you cope. In times of stress, our thinking often becomes impaired and our inner dialogue can become increasingly intrusive. Quite often it is our way of thinking about life that amplifies our heartache. We find ourselves 'generalizing' and 'catastrophizing' our problems, feeling them ripple out and magnify, or we feel a dread of them being never ending.

These tools are designed to help you interpret events in a more balanced way and to chop stress down into manageable pieces. They create a boundary to stress, allowing some breathing space to heal. I encourage you to read over these techniques, work with those that have the most resonance and try the yoga sequence to tap into a feeling of inner strength and peace.

PUT A RING AROUND IT

▶ This remains one the best pieces of advice I have ever received. It helped me get back on track when I was floored by life, and now that life is smoother, I still use it daily. On a simple level, it allows you to focus on one activity or period of time, at a time. In those early months of motherhood when I was overwhelmed by the washing, putting a ring around that task on that occasion, I was able to remind myself that in this moment I have just one load of washing to plough through, not a thousand today, and I could manage this one.

I found myself at the beginning of the recent school summer break freaking out at the thought of how I was going to keep both of my children's needs met for six whole weeks. But the key was to remember I didn't have to do six weeks of mothering at once! Everyone will know how easy it is to get lost in the enormity of tasks that lie ahead, but breaking them down into chunks makes it more manageable. You deal with each day as it comes. Put a ring around this day and tackle it that way, do it hour by hour, or minute by minute when you have to.

'Putting a ring around it' also allows you to isolate a part of your life that is challenging you – maybe you are going through a rough patch in your relationship or there is difficulty in the workplace. This tool helps you recognize that it's not everything, it is just this facet of life that's tough right now. Or perhaps you are facing a turbulent time where lots of different parts of your life feel challenging. You can circle it as an extraordinary period and acknowledge it as such. Even if you can't be certain of its duration, you can find solace in the knowledge that it won't last forever. Putting a ring around a challenging time in your life might allow you to create a little more space to do what you need to do to deal with the current circumstances. It can help you give yourself permission to do more of some things and less of other things, to refine your priorities, to cast aside other burdens until you have greater capacity, and very importantly, to ask others for help and shape how that help is given.

● ● ● ● ● ● ● ●

KNOW YOUR BOUNDARIES

EVERYTHING
WITHIN YOUR
CONTROL

EVERYTHING BEYOND
YOUR CONTROL

▶ This is simple: identify what lies within your control and what lies beyond it. Visualizing the blue circle of control helps me do this. Ask yourself: 'Can I do anything about this?' Pour your energy, effort and attention into what you can control and take action here. Acknowledge where you have no influence. Worrying and wishing are a waste of your time when things lie beyond your power. Get to know your boundaries and feel how this simplifies life, where you direct your attention and your actions. There will be times where there are important things over which we have no control, however, what always lies within our power is how we respond to those events.

MINDFULNESS

▶ Mindfulness helped me bear witness to the painful events unfolding in my life without getting so wrapped up in the chaos and without them becoming part of my identity – we are all more than our story. It created a little space between myself and what was happening in my life and that little bit of distance took away some of the sting. Developing mindfulness, I could observe and accept life as it was with less inner conflict – these things were going to happen anyway, so by just allowing them to be, I was more resourceful in choosing how I could respond.

WHAT IS MINDFULNESS?

▶ Mindfulness is being in touch non-judgementally with the present moment. Our ordinary waking state is one that tends to be jam-packed with reactive thinking, rumination, flitting forwards to what might happen next and diving back into replaying the past. A state without mindfulness is like being on automatic pilot, where all these mental phenomena just happen to us. Rather than being lost in this sea of thought, developing mindfulness puts us back in the driver's seat.

A key concept here is 'non-judgemental'. Practising non-judgemental awareness can be liberating – rather than fighting this moment and then making knee-jerk reactions, we can acknowledge what's happening and how we feel about it, and then make a measured response. It gives us the power to break automaticity and connects us with our inner wisdom.

WHAT MINDFULNESS ISN'T

▶ Mindfulness doesn't mean that you are a passive recipient of life – you still have choices and actions to take. The Mindfulness Tradition recognizes that we are more than our thoughts, feelings, memories and sensations and that who we really are is the witness to these passing states. That in itself can be a very healing concept.

Cultivating mindfulness does not mean that we then don't use our discerning mental capacity. There is a time for being deep in thought, for joyful reminiscing or happy anticipation of something to come. Mindfulness gives us the choice of how and when we harness our minds in a particular way.

WAYS TO DEVELOP MINDFULNESS?

- **Eating mindfully:** Notice what you are eating – the smell, texture and colours. Take a small mouthful, slowly and deliberately exploring every sensation of it.

- **Breathing mindfully:** Feel the sensations of your breathing. Don't try to change it, just breathe normally. Feel the expansion of the inhalation and where it moves through your body. Feel the release of the exhalation as the breath leaves you.

- **Sitting mindfully:** Notice what's unfolding around you. What can you see, what can you hear and what can you smell? Feel the sensations of your body – the grounding of your feet on the floor, the elongation of your spine as the crown of your head lifts skywards. Notice as your mind darts elsewhere and each time it does, bring it back to a non-judgemental experience of sitting.

- **Walking mindfully:** Go for a walk, observing the outer and inner phenomena that unfold. Notice the environment around you, the animals you see, the people, the weather, the greenery, the architecture and watch your inner dialogue. Just witness all these passing phenomena without getting wrapped up in them.

A few deep breaths. Don't do anything, just be with your breath.
This will help you tap into a place of calm and equanimity.
Stick with this stage for as long as you need.

Become aware. Notice what's occurring around you and within you.
You don't have to like what's happening, but notice how resisting it
just adds to your discomfort. Soften your body and let it be as it is.

Choose how you'll respond. Acknowledge that you do have a
choice. Maybe you don't need to do anything right now or maybe
something is required of you. Both compassion and curiosity can
be helpful here. I like to use the phrase 'I wonder...'

coping skills

COMPASSION

▸ While powerful, mindfulness is not enough on its own. It needs to be coupled with compassion. Mindfulness without compassion can feel clinical and overwhelming. Being aware and allowing things to be needs to be couched within a framework of compassion for ourselves and for others.

Compassion is an ability to recognize and see clearly the suffering of others. It is the desire to extend kindness and help towards those who are suffering. It is also a recognition of our common humanity. One of my favourite mantras around compassion is 'We are in it together'. Knowing you're not alone can be very healing, and that feeling of a shared journey can galvanize us to keep going.

HOW DO WE CULTIVATE COMPASSION?

▸ We need to start with ourselves, as difficult as this might seem. Having compassion for yourself is just as important as having compassion for others. We're all familiar with the saying 'you can't love someone else until you've learnt to love yourself,' but just how do we learn to do it? Only talk to yourself as you would your best friend:

- **Observe the way you talk to yourself** (your inner voice and what you vocalize). You can't change something until you are aware of it, so get to know it.

- **Only say things to yourself that would befit your best friend.**

- **When you notice yourself talking harshly, be gentle and appreciate how hard this can be.** Consciously say, 'I'm not doing that to myself any more' and rephrase what you've said. Don't berate yourself.

For many of us, our critical self-talk stems from perfectionism and we think that being hard on ourselves will help us live up to our own expectations. Negative self-talk doesn't enhance performance, confidence, health or well-being. It doesn't make you a better person – it sabotages you. By all means be real – you should evaluate your thoughts, actions and intentions, but do it in a nurturing way.

Time and time again when I've made this suggestion, people report a sense of awakening that changes everything. Kinder self-talk will allow you to deal differently with mistakes, to learn and grow. What I hope you will see blossom is your enjoyment, your self-esteem, patience and a greater ability to respond constructively to the stresses of life.

Another mantra that helps me cultivate a feeling of self-compassion is: 'You are safe, you are loved, you are held.' These were the words that came to me on my yoga mat during pregnancy with baby Ted. As my hands purposefully cradled my abdomen I found myself repeating them to him. I found a deep sense of peace in that connection and it struck me those words were also a great solace to me as an adult. Regardless of age or stage of life, this is what we all need to feel in order to flourish: that we are safe, we are loved and we are held. I also came to realize that as an adult, I need to be able to extend these gifts to myself. The greatest challenges I have faced in my life have all honed this lesson: we must learn to parent ourselves.

If it resonates for you, take a moment to contemplate this mantra. Either sitting or lying, find a comfortable place to rest your hands, close your eyes, relax your breath, soften your body and repeat several times 'I am safe, I am loved, I am held'.

GIVE YOURSELF PERMISSION
TO FEEL AS YOU DO

▸ I made one of the biggest steps on my healing
journey when my counsellor said 'of course you feel
like this'. It was like an enormous burden was lifted
and it helped me go easier on myself. In normalizing
how I felt, I was able to connect with my feelings,
express myself better, and then move through it more
effectively. Giving voice to our feelings helps to bring
them to the surface and allows them to dissipate.

Here's another truth bomb: my goal as a psychologist is not to create perpetually happy people. It's not realistic or helpful to aspire to it. Normal psychological functioning is not an absence of unpleasant feelings! It is normal to experience anxious or depressed thinking at times. They are just thoughts, and it doesn't necessarily follow that you are then 'anxious' or 'depressed'. So, here is the life-changing bit – it's OK to stop trying to eradicate negative thoughts and feelings!

THERE IS A PLACE FOR ALL TYPES OF EMOTION

▶ We're not aiming for happiness all the time, we're aiming for an emotional response appropriate to the situation and one that will help us achieve our desired outcome. All emotions have their place, in fact I no longer use the distinction of positive or negative emotions. Anger might not feel nice, but it helps us protect ourselves and stand up for our beliefs. Grief might also be painful, but it's the natural response to loss, and like sadness, is a call to us to contemplate, slow down and to conserve our energy. Embarrassment is a signal that we've made an error and that some kind of correction is needed. Guilt suggests we've broken our moral code and we need to adjust our behaviour. Doubt prompts us to assess our skills. None of these feelings are particularly comfortable, but they have their healthy place and purpose.

It's OK to stop trying to eradicate negative thoughts and feelings!

Trying to stop, ignore or deny our feelings amplifies our heartache. What helps us find peace is learning how to explore even difficult feelings. Learning to label and interpret your emotions can be transformative – you don't feel it any less, but it helps you move through it more effectively. Look for the presence of more than one emotion or consider other ways of describing what you're feeling. People often come to me with anxiety, but when we take a closer look there are all sorts of other tones in there – excitement, fear, sadness, vulnerability. So many people wind up in my consulting room after suffering a significant loss, saying they don't want to feel like 'this' any more, or they 'shouldn't' feel like this. The crux of it is, they don't need to be fixed and there is nothing to be done to take away their grief. I provide a safe place to express their feelings, and in doing so, those thoughts and emotions are experienced and released. I remind them that sadness is the healthy response to loss and in itself is not a cause for concern. And while it's uncomfortable to experience these emotions, they need to be processed for those feelings to begin to lift and reveal others like profound gratitude, relief and a deep abiding love.

Inherent to human life is an experience of suffering at some stage. We need to allow ourselves to feel these things and know that any attempt to avoid them will only end up amplifying our pain. The only way *out* is *through*. Pain is an inescapable fact of life and essential for our personal growth. Go gently, giving yourself the time and space to feel as you do, and your self-care will help you through.

DEALING WITH UNHELPFUL THINKING

▸ While it's important to allow ourselves to feel as we do, there are times when our thinking can become toxic. Overthinking is where we excessively churn over what we've done or said, or our feelings or problems. We need to address the issues in our life, but overthinking, especially when we are feeling low, seldom helps, in fact it can cause a cascading of unhelpful effects[30], including pessimism and sadness. Rather than going in circles, give your brain something else to anchor on like music, mantras, your breath or exercise – this can help you see more clearly the nub of the issue later and boosts your creativity in generating solutions.

Try writing down your worries. This might help crystallize your thoughts or identify underlying issues. Toss your notes away when you're done so you don't hold onto their negativity. You could talk them over with a friend. Saying out loud what's on your mind brings clarity and can dampen (down) the emotional charge of runaway thoughts. Hearing that others share your feelings can help normalize your situation too. Be mindful not to keep voicing negativity with the same friend – consider their energy bank balance too. Zoom out and ask yourself: 'Will this matter in a year?' If yes, 'What am I learning here or how is this helping me grow?'

REFRAMING ADVERSITY

▶ Grief, coupled with the stress of parenting a newborn, made me feel like I was experiencing some kind of post-traumatic stress syndrome. My eyes were opened to an entirely different concept when I read Martin Seligman's book, *Flourish* – in it he talked about 'Post-traumatic Growth' (PTG). I'd never heard that term before and in an instant, there was an inkling of my experiences being reframed from something solely debilitating to something potentially positive. Just reading about it at the time was a tonic and even now I can see the blossoming that occurred as a result. I hope this concept may provide some help to you, if not right now, perhaps in times to come.

WHAT IS POST-TRAUMATIC GROWTH?

▶ The term PTG was coined by psychologists Richard G Tedeschi and Lawrence G Calhoun in 1995[31] and can be defined as the positive psychological change experienced as a result of the struggle with highly challenging life circumstances. PTG is not simply a return to baseline from a period of suffering; instead, it is an experience of improvement that for some is deeply meaningful. According to research[32], a substantial number of people who display symptoms of depression and anxiety after extreme adversity eventually arrive at a higher level of psychological functioning than before. Amazingly, they found the worse the tragedy, the greater the growth.

It is important to note that I am not saying PTG implies an absence of distress, nor am I passing any comment on these life events in terms of what is right or wrong, fair or unjust; this is just about dealing with what 'is'. These events can cause undeniable hurt, but this can occur at the same time or at least be followed by a sense of growth, expansion and transformation.

If you find yourself in the midst of a traumatic event, these words may seem hollow. The suggestion that anything good could come of your loss may even be downright outrageous, but I urge you to remain open to the possibility. While loss and tragedy are never welcome happenings, at least something of value may come of it in time.

If you feel inspired by the concept of PTG, you could use your Vitality Journal for reflection. The following questions might open your eyes to the silver linings of your experiences: When thinking about your experience, what personal strengths were called upon? How have your relationships developed or how have your bonds deepened? What new doors have opened? Has your sense of appreciation for life itself changed?

MY EXPERIENCE OF PTG

▶ The day after I gave birth, a week after my father's breathing failure and those last goodbyes, I wondered if I'd ever feel whole again. Looking back now, I'd interpret those feelings as my heart being cracked open and deeply awakened – awakened not only to suffering but also to joy, compassion and equanimity.

Through this experience I have become acutely aware of the fragility and preciousness of life. Over the years, once the waves of grief had washed over me (and they still do) I'm finding that this deep sadness is now becoming a profound reservoir of gratitude for my dad – all he brought to this world and all that I'm learning as a result of these experiences.

Now that time and the immediate pain of grief have largely passed, I feel abundant again and the most tangible effect for me is a call to act on my life purpose with courage and conviction. This book is a direct result of my experience of PTG. While it is certainly possible I would have arrived at the same decisions in time, it feels like my loss has propelled me with urgency to live a bigger, more authentic life.

While all things decay and die, from them the velvety petals of our heart unfurl and we can learn to embrace our loss while expressing gratitude for what has come to pass, growing to fully embrace this wonderful life.

The concept of 'seeking the silver lining' is also useful in dealing with the more minor bumps in the road too. Don't be too quick to think of unwanted events as completely negative. In missing out on a much desired school place for my daughter, where she had attended nursery and put down roots, Charlotte and I literally doubled our social connections by making friends at two schools. These are the questions that help me get in touch with the hidden benefits: What good can come from this? What can I learn here? Reflecting on these questions helps me to find a better perspective.

Another enormously useful mantra for finding balance is: How could it be worse? It is easy to get caught up in thinking about how things could be better. When my little ones are ill I try to be mindful of how much worse it could be – we have clarity on their condition, their ailments are relatively minor, they're short-lived, sleep will resume. If I'm feeling stressed about the state of the house – at least I have a roof above my head, and the safety and comfort it provides. It keeps me anchored in a feeling of gratitude and that buoys the spirits so I can dig deeper and carry on.

MANAGING TIME

▶ 'I'm crazy busy' seems to be the modern catch cry.
Try these simple strategies to manage your time.
There are no surprises here – time is a fixed entity, but
the good news is that you have plenty of power over
how you conceive it and parcel it out.

1. Use the 4 Ds

- Do it now – it is important and it must be done by you.

- Defer it – you need to do it, but it can wait. Schedule it
  for later.
- Delegate it – it is important, but someone else can do
  it. Give yourself permission to use this one!
- Dump it – it actually doesn't need to be done.

2. Don't dis the to-do list

The simple act of writing it down helps you process
what's important and what's unnecessary, and frees
up mental energy to actually get things done.

3. Manage distractions

Focus just on the task at hand. If something important
comes to mind, write it down.

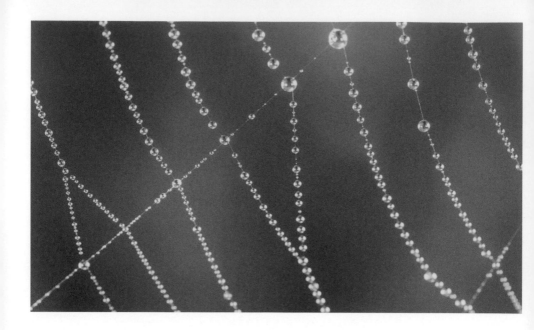

4. Manage your energy

If you're surrounded by half-completed tasks, you might find that this drains your energy for the important stuff. I think of incompletions as punctures in a hose, dissipating the flow of water from where I want to direct it. We've got to plug up those leaks of unfinished business to be effective in dealing with the important things. Identify your incompletions, take action on what you can see through to the end and then relish deleting it from your list. Alternatively, if I am feeling stuck or caught in procrastination, I work on the most inspiring thing on my list to get the energy flowing, and then I return to the item that is most pressing. Know when it's time to take a break despite the temptation to plough on. Remind yourself that taking a moment to replenish can enhance your productivity and effectiveness.

5. Plan your time

If need be, make an appointment with yourself. Do nothing but that particular task for the allotted time.

6. Make peace with imperfection

Identify what needs to be done to the best of your ability and other bits that you can get away with. Acknowledge that you don't have to do everything to the best of your ability. Is it more important to get this one thing done perfectly, or is it better to be on top of all your tasks to a slightly lower standard?

7. Avoid taking on too much

There is only so much time available, so manage your commitments to avoid stress and overwhelm. Where appropriate, remember you can say 'no'. Beware of becoming addicted to 'busyness'. Doing more doesn't always mean you are being productive.

8. Remember to prioritize

Recognize if you're finding it hard to squeeze everything into your week, especially if it is you that keeps on missing out. Say to yourself: 'I have all the time I need'. Feel the space this mantra creates and relax into it. Maybe it will help refine your idea of what actually needs to be done.

little gems ›

These coping tools are designed to help you chop down or reinterpret challenges, giving you space to behave differently while under pressure, to bring perspective to your thinking and to help you process your emotions.

Put a ring around it – circle the task, area of your life or time period to help make life feel more manageable.

Deal with overthinking by eating something nutritious, distracting yourself, jotting it down, saying it out loud, or zooming out!

Know your boundaries – ask yourself 'Can I do anything about this?' If you have no influence over something, no worry, care or action will make a difference, so stop! Place all your energy and effort where you do have control.

Mindfulness – be present to each unfolding moment and allow it to be as it is. Try the A, B, Cs: a few deep breaths, don't do anything just yet. Become aware of what is happening around you and within you. Choose how you'll respond.

Allow yourself to feel as you do. Making space for all feelings, even the uncomfortable ones, is healing. Develop your emotional agility by learning to label your feelings and giving voice to them.

Managing time pressure – do it, defer it, delegate it, dump it. Write it down, plan your time and focus! Is done better than perfect? Give yourself permission to say no! Repeat after me: 'I have all the time I need'.

Compassion – develop kindness and a feeling of shared humanity. Build your skills by working on your self-talk; only talk to yourself as you would your best friend. Connect with the capacity for self-soothing by using the mantra 'I am safe, I am loved, I am held'.

Post-Traumatic Growth – crisis often results in personal growth and transformation. The following questions might open your eyes to the silver linings of suffering: What strengths did you call on? How have your relationships developed? What new doors have opened? Has your sense of appreciation for life itself changed? How have you grown?

YOGA TO HELP YOU COPE IN TIMES OF STRESS, CHANGE & GRIEF

Prayer salute

Begin kneeling with your hands in prayer position at your heart. Inhale and rise up high onto your shins and reach your arms up and overhead, looking up.

Exhale and with control, slowly bring your hands and forehead to the floor and your bottom to your heels in child's pose.

Inhale and come to all fours in cat pose: spine round, your chin towards your chest and your tailbone pointing down towards the floor.

Exhale and come into downward dog, pressing your chest towards your thighs, allowing your head to hang and bringing your heels towards the floor.

Inhale and bring your knees back down to the ground and round your spine again in cat pose.

Exhale and sink your bottom to your heels and your forehead to the floor in child's pose.

Inhale and rise back up onto your shins with your arms extended overhead, keeping your shoulders relaxed away from your ears.

Exhale and come back to kneeling with your bottom on your heels and your hands in prayer position at your heart.

Repeat this sequence three to six times, feeling its soothing effect.

four

PHYSICAL ENVIRONMENT

▶ When I need healing, I turn to Mother Nature. She washes the cells and fibres of my body clean, anchoring me in perspective. I value the tonic of being in nature so much that where possible I take my clients on a 'walk and talk' session rather than sitting in the consulting room. Being in nature enhances problem solving and creativity, it allows us to pause, to find more equanimity. Try it solo, with a friend or the dog – head out for a walk in nature's beauty and see how awe-inspiring it can be. Notice beauty around you and don't get lost in your phone, to-do list or worries.

THE HEALING POWER OF NATURE

▸ For the first few months of Charlotte's life, it seemed the only way she would sleep during the day was while being transported. The baby carrier, pram and car all saw a lot of action. The silver lining to all this enforced movement was that it got me out of my four walls and into nature's beauty. At the time I lived on the beautiful Northern Beaches of Sydney. While I wasn't able to take my solo runs on the beach or my meditative dip in the sea, I was able to push that pram and feel washed clean by the ocean breeze. The majesty of the cliffs helped me channel a sense of calm resolve and the ceaseless tide was reassuring – life goes on and so will I.

The early months of Ted's life weren't terribly different, although we were immersed in a completely different environment. I enjoyed exploring a new terrain in the UK – undulating hills, meadows of wildflowers, open fields, woodland and a ruined castle. The different energetic effects and healing power of nature through the seasons are fascinating.

I call this self-care activity 'Nature Therapy' and I love it because it is free, easily accessible and requires no effort from you beyond noticing it. Granted there are some environments more appealing than others, but wherever you are there will be some natural beauty around you. Take the time to notice it. Maybe it is observing the sky, the wind moving through the trees or the nature we bring inside in the form of cut flowers.

Research showing the therapeutic benefits of nature for mental health and well-being is well documented[33]. Seasonal Affective Disorder, referring to the impact that the changing seasons and availability of natural light have on our well-being, is well known. Horticultural therapy harnesses the therapeutic nature of working with the soil, plants and landscape to promote well-being. It is used in the treatment of anxiety, depression and anger in trauma work with veterans. Getting outdoors is a wonderful self-care activity, either on your own or as a bonding, shared experience with loved ones. Given the frenetic pace of modern life, being in nature reconnects us with simplicity, quiet and a sense of meaning[34].

How to Harness the Therapeutic Power of Nature

- **Make the commitment** to being in nature regularly, immersing all your senses in it and savouring the pleasure of it.

- **Get out in the garden!** You don't need to be skilled to find gardening a deeply rewarding experience. Notice how the plants stand taller and shine after you've given them a good drink of water. Pull up some weeds, rake up the leaves, get down on the ground and see who is living in your garden. Plant your favourite flowers, lovingly tend to them and see them bloom. If you don't have a garden, take a walk and see what grows in your neighbourhood and bring nature inside.

- **Seek out sunshine**, daily if you can – sit in it, notice its warmth, feel the rays being absorbed by your physical body. Imagine you are literally plugging into the sun. Lighting a candle can be a symbolic gesture too. Gaze on it a while and contemplate light for what it means to you.

- **Savour a sunrise or sunset** when you can. Watch it with someone you love and share the experience.

- **Watch the environment** around you, wherever you are – look out of the window while on the bus, while at work, or while you're cooking dinner. Notice birds on the wing, flowers in bloom, leaves turning colour, squirrels looking for nuts or enjoy stroking your pet. Drink it in and enjoy this momentary pause. Feel it filling your cup.

- **Infuse your environment** with more nature – shells, driftwood, pine cones, crystals, rocks, flowers, plants, images. Feature it in the motif of your interior design. Check in with it and feel it lift your spirits.

WORKING WITH YOUR INTERIOR ENVIRONMENT

▸ The environment you are immersed in at home, at work and all the transitions in between have a tangible effect on your well-being. Our individual response to that environment may differ – some people feel at ease in physical mess, for other people a tidy house is literally essential for a 'tidy mind'. We all have our own 'chaos threshold'. Take the time to open your eyes to how your environment is impinging or facilitating your mental clarity and vitality. Even if you think a chaotic environment doesn't bother you, notice how clearing the clutter can free up an enormous amount of energy.

Take a close look at the space around you. Look for aspects of your environment that recharge and inspire you, and savour the enjoyment it brings. On the other hand, look for ways your environment is draining you and take action where possible. Can you create more harmony, order or something more energizing for you?

SIMPLE WAYS TO BE NOURISHED BY YOUR HOME & WORK ENVIRONMENT

▸ Marie Kondo, queen of tidying, says 'putting your house in order is the magic that creates a vibrant and happy life'[35]. There is great wisdom in her approach, which is guided by the ethos of only keeping belongings that spark joy. Consider the places where you spend significant portions of time. How can you beautify this space? It can be as simple as having one treasured keepsake or image that you can rest your eyes upon and feel uplifted.

You can decorate your work environment in simple ways that encourage a feeling of harmony. If you are desk bound, ensure your chair is comfortable and your computer is set up in a way that allows you to relax your neck and shoulders. Keep an image on your desk or set it as a screen saver, use a glass that you enjoy drinking from and choose stationery that inspires you. Even the pleasure of a super-sharp pencil sharpens my thinking.

If you are blessed with plenty of space around you, perhaps you can dedicate a spot for your relaxation. Few of us have the space to dedicate a whole room to it, but maybe there is a chair that you could turn to as your place of well-being. Is there a view to enjoy from your house? This could be a place of nurturing, where you can take a minute to be mindful of your breathing and in doing so recharge your batteries and dissipate any tension.

You can create a space to relax anywhere in your home by forming an intention and setting the scene. When I sit down to write, the only comfortable place is at the dining table, I prepare it first by wiping the surface and lighting a scented candle. Those simple actions clear away the purpose of using that same space for family meals or my daughter's homework and pave the way for my own pursuits.

Love your home and it will love you back. Clean it and tend to it lovingly. Toss away the clutter. Clean the windows so they sparkle back to you and the light can pour in. When I appreciate how cleaning my home facilitates harmony and ease, the act is transformed from drudgery into self-care, especially when I recall that this counts as fine-tuning my fitness! I even engage in a dialogue with my home. I give thanks for the safe haven it provides and in turn it nourishes me. I am grateful for the warm enveloping hug my bed gives me each night. This relationship with my possessions might sound odd, but to me it creates a literal sense of belonging that nourishes me and evokes a feeling of thankfulness, transforming the heaviest of days.

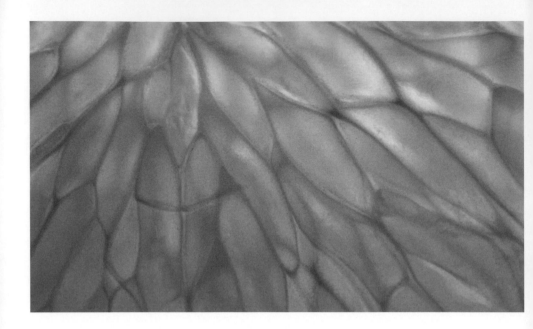

NOURISHING THE SKIN YOU LIVE IN

▶ Cast the notion of vanity aside and groom your way to better health. Allow that nourishment to be an assertion of self-worth and notice how tending to your physical body boosts your self-esteem and well-being. There is nothing selfish about it, just take care of your body and appreciate the dividends. This includes things like enjoying a massage, having a pedicure or going for a haircut. The way I like to bring this type of self-care into action is to look for daily rituals that I can imbue with the intention to nourish myself. That way there is no need to book in for an appointment elsewhere or to fork out for the privilege.

RITUALS OF NOURISHMENT FOR YOUR MIND & BODY

- **As you wake in the morning,** think of one thing that you are looking forward to in your day and let your mind anticipate that for a few breaths. As your feet hit the floor by your bed, give thanks for another day, whatever it holds.

- **As you prepare for the day,** choose an outfit that you feel good in – you're getting dressed anyway, so why not wear things that boost your mood. Cull your wardrobe of items that have the opposite effect.

- **Use a body lotion** that you enjoy the scent of and take the time to massage it mindfully into your limbs, noticing how your body feels, while cultivating gratitude for the physical capabilities of it.

- **A spritz of your perfume** or room spray will enhance your posture and encourage you to take a few deep breaths whenever you need a lift.

- **Choose a hand wash you love,** making a trip to the bathroom an opportunity for nourishment. Take the time to savour the scent.

- **When you return home,** take off your shoes and leave your day behind you. I like to change into a comfortable 'home' outfit. This is not something from my regular wardrobe that I have relegated as something unfit to be seen in, it is something I have chosen specifically for its comfort, that makes me feel good.

little gems ›

Your environment at home, work and the transitions between also have an impact on your well-being. Look for ways to bring more peace, order and harmony into your environment by creating a focal point of something meaningful to you. Let your eye rest there to recharge you.

Invest time in appreciating nature and feel how it helps you reboot. Go for a walk, watch the clouds on your commute or get your hands in the soil in the garden.

Nature has a powerful therapeutic effect, whether you're immersed in the great outdoors or bringing its beauty indoors.

Love your space and it will love you back. The more you care for your environment the more it will nourish you. Clean and clear away clutter to free up your energy.

Nourish the skin that you live in with treatments that keep you free from stress, pain and tension. To make this even more accessible, infuse regular everyday activities with the intention to nurture yourself. Even the simple act of bathing, dressing and your homecoming can be turned into an effective ritual of self-care.

Create a space to relax by setting the scene using scent and visual cues.

notes to myself ▸

YOGA TO HARNESS THE POWER OF NATURE

This sequence can be done outside while on a walk, wearing regular walking shoes, or inside to channel the energy of nature.

Tree

Begin with your feet hip-width apart, toes facing forwards. Take your right big toe to the instep of your left foot, or plant the sole of your right foot against your inner calf or thigh of the left leg. Fully straighten the left leg, pressing the tailbone down towards the floor and taking the right knee out wide and angling it down to the floor. Keep your hips and chest square. Extend your arms up and out above you in a 'V' shape. Breathing smoothly here, elevate the crown of your head skywards as you send roots down through your standing foot. (Sense of humour essential!) Hold for 5–15 breaths and repeat on the other side.

Spine rolls

Stand with your feet hip-width apart, your knees bent and hands placed on your thighs. With your head heavy, drop your chin towards your chest. Feel your arms go floppy like a rag doll and roll down into a forward bend with very bent knees. Lengthen the spine from both ends, feeling your tailbone and the crown of your head descend towards the floor. Hang out in the forward bend for 5–10 breaths and then slowly begin to roll back up, stacking one vertebra on top of the other, rebuilding your posture from your pelvis up to your shoulders, neck and lastly your head. Repeat a few times, growing taller every time you roll back up.

Mountain breaths

Stand with your feet hip-width apart, your arms by your sides, gazing forwards. Inhale and reach your arms out and up overhead, gazing up towards your thumbs. Exhale and lower your arms back down and gaze forwards. Feel the fullness of your breathing and enjoy growing taller with every repetition.

five

▶ Moving from one side of the globe to the other while pregnant, to a town where I knew no one, I knew I needed to build a healthy support network as quickly as possible. Notice that this chapter is about 'connection' in general and not just relationships. This experience of starting afresh in a new place taught me just how much incidental connection with strangers can feed the soul. While I was in the process of meeting people and building friendships, it was the happy interactions with the lovely lady who made my morning coffee, the women at the grocery store and the casual encounters with other parents in the playground that kept me going. It could've been a terribly lonely time and while I hungered for time with a dear old buddy, I could still feel a sense of connection and belonging by sharing an experience with someone I'd just met.

So be on the lookout for these opportunities to connect and don't be afraid to make yourself vulnerable. What amazed me was the kindness that

I experienced when I reached out to people, the warm reception I was given when I explained I was new in town. Even now that I have many strong friendships to support me, I still enjoy the sense of belonging created by talking and sharing with the people I meet incidentally in my day. Look for appropriate ways that you can 'plug in' during your day.

SOCIAL CONNECTION & WELL-BEING

▶ There is no denying the profound effect that social connection, or its absence, has on our well-being. Humans have a basic need to belong – it is an evolutionary, biological drive. Our relationships provide us with support in times of crisis and they amplify our joy in the good times. In connecting with others we experience love, comfort and acceptance, adding meaning and purpose to our lives. Connection sets into motion that upward spiral of positivity: the more time, energy and effort we put into building more positive connections, the more we experience positive emotions. Investing in social connection is one of the most powerful self-care strategies for boosting your well-being.

CONNECTION DURING CRISIS

▶ If you're in the midst of a very stressful time, it can be difficult to maintain relationships as you might normally do so. Sometimes, being in the company of others or particular people can feel draining. Give yourself permission to do what you need to do at this time. Maybe you see more of some people and less of others. Maybe you choose to spend your time with people doing different activities. If you, like me, have a tendency to isolate yourself when you are feeling low, remind yourself of the value of connection and reach out to people in a way that feels doable. If help is offered to you, give yourself permission to shape how that help is given.

WAYS TO CREATE CONNECTION & BOOST YOUR RELATIONSHIPS

GET IN TUNE WITH OTHER PEOPLE

▶ This is precisely the skill we need to make the most out of those incidental opportunities to connect. Become aware of the people you come into contact with during your day and be present to that opportunity to connect. Give them eye contact, listen to them, communicate an interest in what they are saying and ask them questions. Just by drawing your awareness to the quality of the attention you give to others, you better create a sense of closeness[36].

CELEBRATE THE GOOD STUFF!

▶ This is about showing genuine pleasure in hearing the good fortune of other people. How we respond to people when they're sharing their good news can either build our connection or undermine it[37]. 'Active and constructive responding' is where you demonstrate a real interest, seek more information about what happened by asking questions, encourage the other person to relive the event with you and reflect back that you share their joy, if that's how you genuinely feel. At the other end of the continuum there is 'passive-destructive' and 'active-destructive' responding where respectively the good news is ignored or the response given is openly critical or dismissive. If active and constructive responding doesn't come naturally to you, remember it is a skill that you can cultivate. Notice how people respond to you as your skill grows. You are likely to find that people like you better and want to be in your company more often. You're likely to find that it will boost your energy, self-esteem and confidence.

SHOW YOU CARE

▸ A place to start with developing your caring capacity can be looking at the ratio of positive to negative statements you make. It's important for the health of your relationships to balance expressions of gratitude and affection with criticism. When we start to pay attention to the tone of our regular dialogue many people are staggered by their current positive to negative ratios. Research has shown that to sustain a relationship you need a minimum of three positive statements for every critical statement and if you want your relationships to flourish, aim for a ratio of 5:1[38]. There is a point of diminishing returns though: above 13:1 and you lose your credibility. The praise or positive feedback needs to be genuine for this ratio to hold. Start by noticing what you are saying and practise bringing that ratio into a healthy balance. I also try to counter negative thoughts because even if those sentiments aren't verbalized they leak out

- in other ways. Try looking for kinder attributions to behaviour and focus on the strengths of your loved ones rather than their foibles.

- Look for opportunities to be caring and to acknowledge kindness that you receive. Many a tense moment can be transformed by a kind act or loving touch. The way that we communicate has a huge impact on how that information is understood. It's not just the tone of what is said, it is the specific words we choose. Try to use 'I' statements that make your position or feelings clear rather than using 'you' statements that accuse the other person. It is helpful to refer to specific situations or behaviours rather than exaggerating and generalizing by saying 'always' or 'never'. As a listener we can communicate care and kindness by being quiet, maintaining eye contact and taking in what is being said without interruption. The questions you ask as a listener also demonstrate care, for example reflecting back what you have heard and asking whether you have understood accurately. The listener can also ask if there is anything else to say or whether there is something to be done. Communicating is not always about problem solving – sometimes all that is desired is to be heard.

- In the midst of conflict, this is the mantra I use: 'Don't be THE bigger person, be A bigger person'. This helps me to take my ego down a notch, dials down the feeling of opposition and reminds me of the person I aspire to be. Even counting to ten before responding can dissipate those stress hormones, and remember, a solution is better than being right!

PRIORITIZE YOUR RELATIONSHIPS

▸ Even when life is very full, make time to connect. Maybe the way you connect might change for that period of time, but make an effort to stay current. Make time to talk and to listen on a regular basis. We can connect with our friends and loved ones via the small, everyday things as well as a sense of shared rituals, dreams and goals. These are the things that bind us together and help create a feeling of belonging.

I like to send my mum in Australia a photo of a moment in my day accompanied by a brief message to share that experience with her – it doesn't take much time but I feel closer to her in the process.

Another favourite is sharing a 'gratitude dinner' with my family or friends. This is where we come together with the express intention of sharing love and appreciation, to celebrate successes, and where we deliberately choose to steer away from talk of problems or stresses. Ensure you are all in the mood for it and can make the commitment to this intention, otherwise it won't work.

WE ALL NEED A TEAM!

▶ I like to think I have a whole team of people on my side. Who's on yours? This is worth reflecting on and writing down. Who do you share the journey with and who are the people or practitioners that help put you back together when crisis hits? To get you thinking I'll let you know who's on mine: a walking companion, yoga buddies, a kind ear, a mindfulness friend, my osteopath, my coaching psychologist mentor, my beauty therapist, my hairdresser, coffee mates, playground pals, a brainstormer and sometimes devil's advocate, and a cheer squad – on social media and in real life (both have their value). This is my team of angels: people who pamper and fix me, who keep me honest on my path, who lift me up when I'm flagging, who inspire me, challenge me and celebrate my wins with me.

When I need a boost, I just check out my list and all the names are there for easy reference. I can take action faster. I can make a better decision on who to reach out to – my team members have different strengths so I choose to connect with the person who can help me most in this current situation. I can also take a peek at my list and see who I haven't connected with for a while and make the effort to reach out. Get your angels on speed dial, share the good times with them and draw on them when times get tough. Relish being on their team too.

In my experience all of these strategies tend to be largely common sense and will occur quite naturally when we are feeling energetic and when the flow of life is smooth and easy. However, when the going gets tough these skills can get lost in the chaos and we can alienate ourselves just when we need the support and nourishment from close relationships the most. When we find ourselves in this kind of place, just touching base with these techniques can help us find our way back to a more fruitful way of relating to our loved ones and to promote healing later on.

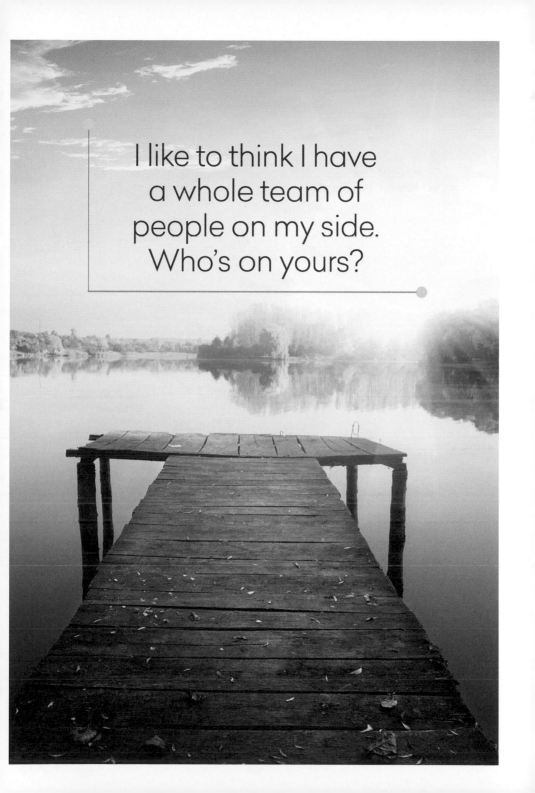

little gems ▸

▸ Connecting with other people is deeply nourishing, whether they are close friends or strangers. It provides a sense of shared experience, common humanity and belonging, which feed the soul.

▸ Developing your skills of connection and boosting the positivity of your relationships are powerful self-care activities.

▸ Celebrate the wins and boost the health of your relationships. When a loved one shares good news with you, give it your full attention and ask them to relive the event with you and squeeze all the enjoyment out together.

▸ Take the heat out of conflict with the mantra: 'Don't be THE bigger person, be A bigger person'. Your relationships provide fertile ground for personal growth and evolution once your ego gets out of the way.

▸ Connect with people by getting in tune with them. Work on your listening skills, giving eye contact, and showing an interest by asking questions.

▸ Who's on your team? Take a moment to reflect on the special people in your life, write them down and consider the role you play in each other's lives. Draw on them for support and enjoy offering yours to them.

▸ Show you care by bringing your positive to negative comments to a ratio of 5:1. Soften your language by referring to how you feel and specific events rather than attacking the other person's character with 'you' statements or generalizing. Learn how to listen with care, paying attention, asking questions and asking what the other person needs.

▸ Give your relationships genuine priority, make time for them and aim to stay current.

YOGA TO HARNESS THE POWER OF CONNECTION

Circular sun salute

Stand with your feet hip-width apart, your knees soft and your hands placed on your thighs. Inhale and lift your arms forwards and upwards, looking up. Exhale and lower your hands down through the centre of your body through prayer pose, hinge forwards at your hips and place your fingertips on the floor. Inhale and keeping your knees soft, sweep your arms in a circle to the right, all the way back to upright. Exhale and continue the circle back down to the floor. Inhale and change direction, circling to the left. Exhale and return to the centre with your fingertips on the floor. Inhale and come back up to standing, bringing your hands through the centre line of your body and reach them overhead. Exhale and separate your hands and bring them back down to your sides, enjoying a chest stretch on the way.

Dynamic warrior lunge

Stand at the back of your mat with your feet hip-width apart, like you're standing on train tracks. Take a giant step forwards with your right foot, staying on those train tracks. Bend your right knee deeply and straighten your back leg – the back heel will remain off the floor. Staying in the lunge, bring your hands to your heart in prayer mudra. As you inhale, stretch your arms out wide to the sides like albatross wings. As you exhale, bring your hands back to your heart. On the next breath in, reach your arms up and overhead into a 'V' shape and look upwards.

As you exhale, bring your hands back to your heart and gaze forwards. Repeat the arm movements 3–6 times before changing legs.

Dynamic horse pose with lotus mudra

Stand with your feet one and half times your shoulder-width apart. Angle your toes out to 45 degrees. To form the petals of the lotus, bring your wrists, thumbs and little fingers together and stretch your fingers wide apart. To create the roots of the lotus bring your fingertips towards each other, curl your fingers in towards your palms and the back of your hands towards each other, stretching your fingertips now towards the inner forearm. As you breathe in, straighten your legs and reach your hands upwards in lotus flower mudra, looking up towards your hands. As you breathe out, form the roots of the lotus, bend your knees deeply into a squat and gaze forwards. Repeat this 6–10 times, feeling the strength of your legs, focusing on the mudra and how this helps you feel plugged in.

Finish with some shoulder rolls. As you breathe in raise your shoulders up towards your ears. As you breathe out, roll your shoulders back and down. Repeat 5 times, keeping your arms, eyes and jaw relaxed.

SIX

MOOD BOOSTERS

▸ What we watch has a potentially huge impact on our mood. I made the mistake of indulging in *Days of our Lives* when baby Charlotte was sleeping and I can tell you, if you're not depressed before watching it you're likely to be after. This pathway of the Vitality Wheel is all about the simple ways we can boost our mood. I love this pathway because it contains many of the activities and skills that genuinely don't take much time. Some don't require any extra time because they are teaching you to harness your mind more constructively – you are thinking, seeing and perceiving all the time, you might as well get your brain on side!

As you embark on using this spoke of the Vitality Wheel it is helpful to recall the concept of the energy bank. Take stock of your day and observe the things that naturally top you up energetically – try to do more of these things. Notice as well the things that tend to deplete you. Some of these things are unavoidable and in those circumstances we use self-care to make up for the deficit. You may, however, find there are some things that you can minimize or avoid altogether – please give yourself the permission to make these choices and take good care of your energy bank balance.

MOOD-BOOSTING ACTIVITIES

Music

Listen to whatever helps your spirit soar. Couple it with an activity you don't love so much or that you find stressful and you might find that music can transform the way you feel about it. I like to have some uplifting pop on while I'm getting the kids ready for school, while classical music definitely helps me if the traffic is heavy or I'm running late. If you enjoy it, have a good sing or dig out that instrument.

Clothing

Pop on your favourite clothes or wear a colour you find uplifting. Maybe it's just a swoosh of a lippy that you love. I have a necklace that belonged to my grandmother. Wearing it makes me feel a sense of closeness and it's one of my favourites for that reason. Choose mindfully what you dress yourself in and imbue those actions with a feeling of self-love.

Scent

I enjoy using perfume, room sprays and candles, and find that coupling scent with an intention is really powerful. I light a carefully chosen scented candle while Ted has his nap and tie that in with the intention for how I am going to use that prized time. Enjoy exploring how different fragrances can cultivate different moods.

Laughter

Watch a funny movie, show or clip, or do something that gives you a lift or makes you chuckle. Get some laughter in your day. And don't underestimate the power of YouTube cat videos!

Play

Hobbies are a wonderful way to engage the mind and boost your mood. Jigsaws, mind puzzles, card or board games – there are some really wonderful things available these days. If you're a 'birdvert', you'll love bird bingo as much as my family does. Or just get down on the floor and roll about with your pet or children.

Expand your mind

Learn a new skill, try out a new sport, prepare a new dish or just eat something new to you. What are you curious about? Explore the world and immerse your senses in what you find awe-inspiring. We have so many great resources at out fingertips. I'm a fan of sitting down with a good podcast or TED talks.

Creativity

There is a plethora of ways you can get your 'craft on' that helps the happies flow. Check out the explosion of colouring books for adults, try origami or grab a pencil and draw. Just enjoy being playful and express yourself. If you prefer, go and appreciate great art instead.

Beauty

Seek out anything you find awe-inspiring, natural or man-made, and feel how this lifts your energy. You will find some kind of beauty to appreciate just about anywhere you are, if not, close your eyes and use the power of your imagination.

Look up!

The simple act of looking up changes how we feel. There is some fascinating research from psychologist Erik Peper examining the relationship between our body position and how we feel[39]. The way we sit, stand and hold our bodies has been shown to have a powerful impact on our mood and energy levels. Research by Peper shows that being hunched or slumped reduces our subjective energy levels, lowers mood, aids the recall of negative memories and stimulates crying. Elongating the spine and opening the chest boosts your mood, promotes feelings of vitality and enhances recall of positive events. In fact, this upright and open posture can make it difficult to remember negative events and makes it harder to cry. Watch your posture and notice how it affects how you feel. Try out the yoga sequence at the end of this chapter (see pages 170–171). Need more convincing? Google Amy Cuddy and her inspiring TED talk on 'power postures'.

Seek out anything you find awe-inspiring, natural or man-made, and feel how this lifts your energy.

MOOD-BOOSTING SKILLS

SAVOURING

▸ This is one of my all-time favourite mood boosters. Get good at savouring and you will have instant access to positivity. Savouring can be described as thoughts or actions that create, amplify and sustain enjoyment. This is where you notice a pleasurable experience, you give it your full attention, you immerse yourself in all the enjoyable things about it, feeling it as intensely as possible and you let the experience linger as long as possible.

There are three different components to savouring – past, present and future. You can savour the past by reminiscing with a buddy over a shared happy memory. You can savour the present by immersing yourself in the pleasure of the moment at hand, like a good cup of coffee, feeling its warming effects, taste and aroma. You can savour the future by joyfully anticipating and visualizing what might lie ahead, like that long-awaited summer holiday. Cultivate this fantastic skill of savouring and don't let a moment of joy escape you!

GRATITUDE

▸ Gratitude is the other great mood alchemist. Learn to cultivate this attitude of thanks and your experience of life will be transformed. Gratitude is a feeling of counting your blessings, giving thanks or simply feeling a sense of appreciation and wonder. It is closely related to savouring, and grateful thoughts can help you to savour positive life experiences. You can think of gratitude as the antidote to emotions such as jealousy, worry and irritation, and it is much broader and more powerful than just saying 'thank you'. The practice of gratitude focuses on the present moment, on appreciating your life or this moment as it is and for what has made it so.

My favourite way of cultivating this skill is taking what I call a 'gratitude walk' – this is where you head outside with the express intention to just count your blessings. Don't let your mind wander to worry or thoughts of those that you perceive to have more than you. If it does, hunt down those silver linings and acknowledge those that are not as fortunate as you. Notice all the things around you that bring you joy. Think of all the things in your life right now for which you are thankful. Reflect on the small things in your day that have gone well. Think of events in your life that have opened doors. Think of ways that you are growing and cultivate a deep feeling of gratitude for what is, what has been and what might be. You can also do this exercise inside and sitting down, in fact you can do it anywhere and anytime.

There are other methods too for fine-tuning this skill. Another option is to write a gratitude letter or make a gratitude phone call. Expressing gratitude face to face, in a letter or over the phone can be extremely powerful. Think of someone to whom you owe a debt of gratitude and express in concrete terms what you are thankful for. Be detailed about what they did for you and how it has enriched your life. It is also good practice to counter ungrateful or disparaging thoughts – simply acknowledge when these thoughts arise and consciously counter them with kinder, more grateful ones or simply try to look at the situation in a different way, with a more benevolent perspective.

TRY A LITTLE KINDNESS

▸ Kindness needs little introduction, we all know what it means. What is helpful to point out is that practising acts of kindness can invigorate, uplift and forge strong positive connections between people. Kindness sets that upward spiral of joy firmly into action. So the next time you feel you need a little boost, think less about what others can do for you and more about how you can be of service to others.

Is there someone that needs your help today? How can you make a contribution? Can you soften your interpretation of someone else's behaviour? I find the mantra 'hurt people hurt people' helps me to cultivate kindness when I'm dealing with loved ones who are being prickly or difficult. It reminds me to be loving towards them even in their least lovable moments!

Showing kindness can be as simple as a smile, going with someone else's preference, being extra courteous on the road or showing more attentiveness to your teenager's story. Challenge yourself to do things that don't necessarily come naturally and feel how it is an opportunity to grow. Do someone a good turn without any expectation of anything in return. Feel how it warms your heart. Extend that kindness to yourself as well! You know that inner critic? It's time to make peace.

LEARN THAT YOU ARE ENOUGH

Do any of these sound familiar?

- I'm not good enough.
- I don't know enough.
- I'm not strong enough.

The list goes on... What is the statement that rears its head for you? We all have at least one. One niggly refrain that repeatedly voices itself. In case you're wondering, mine is the 'I don't know enough'.

What I am learning is that I don't necessarily have to silence these statements; I can make peace with them. Something along the lines of 'feel the fear and do it anyway'. Let's go right to the heart of all these 'I am not enough' statements. I want to share some insight with you in the hope that it can start to lessen the potency of your particular phrase.

This is what I want you to know, not just on an intellectual basis, but a cellular basis – by that I mean I want it to sink into every cell and fibre of your being. I want you to sit with these words, drink them in, repeat them internally, out loud if that suits, and let them truly percolate:

- You are already enough.

- You are already whole.

- You are already perfect.

- Every living being is already whole, perfect and complete – it was given freely to you with your miraculous creation.

- There is no hole to fill, nothing to fix, nothing to be done.

We just need to remember what we have forgotten, or denied or been told otherwise. I have come to learn this in my own personal healing journey, but also in working with many, many other people in their journey to wellness. It is a constant echo with my clients, both young and old, this notion that somehow we are not enough. It strikes at the heart of even the most brilliant people. It can keep eating away at you until you learn to really embrace deeply the sentiments above. There is no university degree, no career, no grade, no other personal accomplishment that will magic away that doubt or fill that hole... you just need to grasp that there is in fact, no hole to fill.

How do we make peace with these nagging statements of self-doubt? Here's a process to try:

1. Get to know your phrase

You might have one, you might have a couple. What is it that niggles at you?

2. Notice it

Just be aware of it every time it taps you on the shoulder.

3. Make room for it

This is the trickier bit. Learn to make peace with it. With practice, every time you notice it, greet it with a smile, like it's an old friend. Welcome it with tenderness – think of it as an old cardigan that you wear from time to time, 'you old thing'. Let it be there around your shoulders and don't try to shrug it off. Maybe just by noticing it and not wriggling away from it, it might slip from your shoulders on its own. If it stays put, just breathe your way through it and carry on. When my phrase of 'not knowing enough' pops up, instead of it getting in my way, I use it as a reminder of how much I value wisdom and keeping my knowledge current. It propels me to dig deeper, keep growing and learn more.

4. Get on with it

Acknowledge that this is just a collection of words, just a thought. It is not the truth and it certainly does not have to be a barrier. This is the technique that helps me get on with it: I imagine that there are a bunch of different personalities to my thoughts, each with their own voice. Many of them you'll know already – there's the inner critic, the inner child, the inner cheerleader and the inner elder. (I urge you to get to know your inner elder, that white-haired version of you smiling back and saying 'it's going to be OK!' Just being aware of the concept has allowed me to hear my inner elder's voice better – she often offers a word of consolation, she reminds me of ways I have coped before and she helps me cut to the chase with the action that's going to help in this moment.) I allow all these characters to have their say but I hold an imaginary microphone up to the voice that's going to support me through the doubts and fears. It's not about being fearless or having all the answers, it's about showing up and stepping up regardless.

Is there a place for evaluating ourselves? Absolutely. But it does not lie in debating our worth as human beings. It does not lie in assessing our achievements, our awards, the number of friends we have, the size of our house, the car we drive or our bank balance. In my experience, these are more useful questions to ponder:

- **Are you living your truth?**

- **Are you living a life imbued with personal meaning?**

- **Are you living a life inspired by your own unique strengths, gifts and talents?**

- **Are you living a life guided and shaped by your own personal values?**

little gems ›

▸ Add to your self-care toolkit some mood-boosting activities, including music, your clothing, scent, things that make you laugh, artistic pursuits, looking up, opening up your posture and looking out for anything that inspires awe.

▸ Develop your mood-boosting skills by savouring life's joys, reminiscing over happy memories, immersing yourself in a pleasurable moment and anticipating a joyful future event. Double your joy by savouring with a buddy.

▸ Transform the quality of your day by expressing gratitude with a simple thank you or by taking a gratitude walk. Count your blessings. Ask yourself 'What went well today?'

▸ Quit trying to silence your inner critic – pass the mic to your inner elder or inner cheerleader instead.

▸ Try the mantra: 'You are already enough. You are already whole. You are already perfect. Every living being is already whole, perfect and complete – it was given freely to you with your miraculous creation. There is no hole to fill, nothing to fix, nothing to be done.'

▸ Practise kindness to uplift your spirits. How can you be of service to others? Even the smallest act of kindness can be a mood alchemist. Extend that kindness to yourself as well.

notes to myself ›

MOOD-BOOSTING YOGA

High lunge

Stand at the back of your mat, feet hip-width apart on your 'train tracks'. Take a giant step forwards with your right foot, staying on those train tracks. Bend your right knee deeply and straighten your back leg – the back heel won't reach the floor. Inhale and reach your arms up and overhead to a 'V' shape. Exhale and bend your elbows, arms forming a 'W' shape. Repeat six times before changing legs. This sequence is uplifting and enlivening.

Mountain calf raise

Stand with your feet hip-width apart and your palms on your outer thighs. Inhale and stretch your arms out and upwards as your heels lift simultaneously. Keep gazing forwards. Exhale and at the same time, with control lower your arms and lower your heels, both touch their starting position simultaneously... this is easier said than done! Keep your shoulders and jaw relaxed. Repeat six times.

Dynamic standing twist

Stand with your feet shoulder-width apart. Swing both of your arms around to the right-hand side, twisting your body in the same direction, then repeat to the other side. Let your arms be floppy and relaxed. Twist at least six times to each side, enjoying the freedom and lightness of this movement.

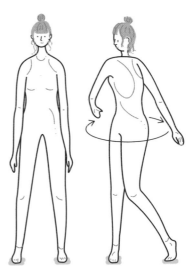

seven

▶ 'Find a happy person and you will find a project'[40]. These are wise words from pioneering positive psychologist Sonja Lyubomirsky and I think she's onto something. Learning how to set effective goals is an essential ingredient of bringing any of the Vitality Wheel pathways into action. If you want to clean up your eating, move more, develop a better sleep routine, find time to relax, see your mates more often or plan a holiday. Setting a goal will help you achieve all of these things. If you put this book down with just one goal, please let it be the intention to nourish yourself daily with some form of self-care.

If you want to achieve any kind of change in life, whether that be integrating a new healthy habit, getting back on your feet after adversity or making a bold career move, setting a goal will help you take action. Research clearly shows you are more likely to make it happen if you set yourself a goal around it[41]. Goals help to structure your time and give shape to your life. They fine-tune your awareness, give you a sense of drive and staying power, and help you take action consistent with your values. Research also shows that people who have a commitment to something personally significant are happier than those without firm aspirations[42].

If the thought of making goals leaves you cold, hold on. There are some really simple goal-setting principles that could transform how you feel about goals and how effective they can be. While the right goals uplift you, poorly crafted goals can demotivate you. Before you set any goals, be honest with your energy levels and the demands you are facing in life right now. If the idea of brainstorming a goal feels like it is just adding to your burden, then perhaps soften the concept by forming an 'intention' – maybe it could be a simple commitment to one daily act that enhances your well-being, or maybe the goal is just to get through this day, or when it's really tough, get through this hour. I often hear people say they just don't have time to set goals and if you fall into this camp, then my cautionary words would be to expect little in life to change... if you want to create any meaningful shift it is unlikely to happen on its own and a goal will help you grow.

When I was at my lowest ebb, my goals had to be simple – like committing to five minutes of yoga a day. The overarching goal of Charlotte's early years was to get back on my feet and be the best mum I could in the circumstances. It wasn't the time to launch into setting grand goals about what lay further ahead than that.

Even second time around with Ted, when I had a little more energy for a sense of humour, I would jokingly say the goal of that period was to 'blink and breathe'! Once I felt like the energy was flowing a little better and there was space to take on more, it was time to revisit my longer-term goals. I enjoyed focusing on returning to work, investing more time in my relationships and taking a good look at boosting my physical health. There is a time for everything, but we can't necessarily do it all at once. Choose your focus wisely.

My big dream for this year is to make a return visit to Sydney and show Ted the beaches where I spent my childhood. This is a challenging goal in terms of financial planning and without clearly articulating this desire, making the collective commitment to this goal and taking determined action, it just won't be possible. I love how this goal helps simplify decision making – every time my six-year-old spies another item she is desperate for I ask her, 'What would you rather – this itty bitty thing that will entertain you for five minutes or would you prefer to take Grandma back to Taronga Zoo in Australia?' On a tough day I can anticipate the achievement of this goal and it helps to put a little pep in my step to keep working at it.

There is a time for
everything, but we
can't necessarily do
it all at once.

HOW TO SET ATTAINABLE GOALS

▸ So how do you craft the kind of goals that motivate and uplift you? Lyubomirsky[43] describes five key characteristics of goals that work best to enhance our well-being. They are:

1. Intrinsic

Goals that are personally rewarding and inspiring to you as opposed to 'extrinsic' goals, which are a reflection of what other people want for you, what you think you should do or goals imposed on you.

2. Authentic

Goals that are anchored in your own values, interests and beliefs, and those that fit with your personality and natural strengths. If you're not sure how to clarify your values and strengths, leap over to the chapter on Values and Purpose (see pages 192–207). Your goals need to tap into something you truly care about. Motivational speaker Simon Sinek puts it eloquently: 'Working hard for something we don't care about is called stress; working hard for something we love is called passion'. To illustrate, last year I failed massively at my goal to 'improve my cooking'. Why? Because as an activity in itself, I don't particularly care about cooking. That resolution failed to propel me into action. When I take a closer look at what the art of cooking facilitates in my life, I start to tap into its value and I feel a stirring of excitement: I want to prepare healthy

and life-giving meals for myself and my family. I want my children to learn how to prepare nourishing food for themselves. I want to be an authentic well-being practitioner, living the suggestions I offer to my tribe. Seen through this lens, cooking becomes an essential activity to living in accordance with what's really important to me. So the goal becomes 'prepare more nourishing food and involve my children in the process' and I am galvanized into action.

3. 'Approach' rather than 'avoid'

Frame your goals positively so that they involve becoming or approaching a desirable outcome rather than avoiding an undesirable outcome. Your goals act as powerful primer statements to your brain, so a goal to 'eat less chocolate' will have your brain focusing on... chocolate! A more effective goal would be to carve a new ritual of pleasure, such as a savoured cup of tea.

In my experience, when we shift the goal from something like 'lose weight', to 'daily self-care to boost vitality', we start getting into great shape and making better lifestyle choices naturally. When you're happy, energetic and well, negative thought patterns and unhelpful behaviours tend to drop away by themselves. Research backs up this notion that when we commit to values that aren't directly related to weight loss that's when we often experience weight loss[44].

4. Harmonious

Make sure that your intentions complement each other rather than conflict with each other. One of the most frustrating periods of my life was when Teddy was very little and my two goals were 'be there for Ted' and 'build a business'. These competing goals were a fabulous recipe for inner conflict and until I achieved some resolution between them, I felt terribly stuck. Sometimes we have to 'park' goals until conditions become more favourable or we reign in a particular goal to make space for another one. It helps to zoom out and be honest with ourselves about what is reasonable and achievable right now. It's worth acknowledging too that it in relationships it certainly helps to have harmony between your goals and those of your significant other. Perhaps it's not possible for you to simultaneously pursue your goals right now. I think the concept of turn taking can be helpful here.

5. Reasonable and flexible

Take into account your current circumstances and available resources. These variables can change, so we need to keep our goal setting fluid. Rigid goals create another recipe for inner conflict, so allow there to be some wiggle room for your evolving circumstances.

ACHIEVING YOUR GOALS

GETTING INTO THE RIGHT HEADSPACE

▸ Make sure you are in the right frame of mind before brainstorming your goals. When you feel ready, jot down in your Vitality Journal what you want to achieve. Don't limit yourself by feeling you have to know how these things will happen just yet. Using the five guidelines on pages 176–178, formulate some goals – the clearer and more specific, the better, and give them a loose timeframe. Don't just think about it, write it down. The act of recording your goals is an important step in making a psychological contract with yourself. Once you've chosen your goals mindfully (you'll know your goals are right for you if thinking about them stimulates a feeling of excitement or positivity), you then need to brainstorm some action steps. It's not enough just to think about your goals; to achieve any change you have to take action.

FOLLOWING THROUGH

▸ Once you've worked out what you want, you need to work out how you're going to do it. Brainstorm the actions or behaviours required to move you towards

your goal. For example, if your goal is to boost your physical fitness, what specific action does this require? What do you need to do more of or what new behaviours do you need to engage in to bring your goal to life? Write down three action steps you can take now to progress you towards achieving your goal – it might be calling a friend and making a date to go for a walk together. Maybe it is purchasing a pair of walking shoes. Once you've completed your actions, what's next on your list? Write them down and make the commitment to yourself. Remember to place a tick on your calendar for every day you take a positive step towards your goal – once you've started you won't want to miss a day.

BREAK IT DOWN

▸ Chop your end goal down into smaller subgoals – think of these as the mini milestones you can celebrate, boosting your self-esteem along the way. This can be an effective way to break inertia and avoid feeling overwhelmed. I began writing this book when Ted was born. The goal to 'write a book' while tending to a new-born was potentially nuts, but it was a way of making my goals for motherhood and professional life mutually attainable. I wrote while he slept and by breaking the project down into steps, this book came to life. First it was thinking about what I wanted to write about, then it was organizing my thoughts, writing the manuscript, researching the publishing world, finding an agent, securing a publisher and here it is! Those bite-sized chunks were essential for keeping things manageable. It also helps to ponder some rewards for achieving each of your steps. Just make sure you choose something life-giving that doesn't sabotage your efforts in the long run!

CONSIDER OBSTACLES & WAYS TO OVERCOME THEM

▸ Think of any potential obstacles you might encounter along the way – time, energy, funds, resources and knowledge. If any of these barriers seem immovable, can you rejig your goal or rework your timeframe so it is more attainable? Proactively determining ways to overcome potential challenges will have you bouncing back into action sooner. Primer statements can be useful in navigating these curveballs. For example, if I have to work late and miss my gym class, then I will do my ten-minute home workout routine. Have a plan and you'll feel empowered even in the midst of a setback.

CALL ON YOUR TEAM

▶ Draw on other people for support. Say it out loud and make your commitment known to the people around you. This will help the significant others in your life understand your priorities and help you rather than unknowingly sabotage you in your goal pursuit. Consider enlisting a buddy for mutual support, someone that shares your passion or shares your drive to achieve something personally important and work on your goals together. Maybe it is just a friend who wants to see you thrive who you can call on to keep you honest.

Consider turning to a coach for support – a partner to brainstorm with, someone who is impartial, who will check in with you, enhancing that feeling of accountability. After all, we don't think twice about using a personal trainer to help us with our fitness goals. Perhaps there are some gaps in your knowledge, so turn to an expert in that field and seek the answers you need. You are far more likely to succeed with the support of people around you, so share your goals and let them assist!

CHECK IN, FINE TUNE & CELEBRATE

▶ Keep revisiting your goals at defined intervals, refining them, prioritizing them and reaffirming your commitment. This harnesses the other benefit of goal setting – celebrating our accomplishments! Too often we leap straight onto the next hurdle to tackle. Take the time to acknowledge your mini milestones and celebrate with your team. I love sitting down with my Vitality Journal and taking stock, looking over goals I've set and reflecting on progress. Sometimes I am yet to achieve that particular aim, but I can still celebrate how far I've come. Sometimes I am able to cross them off and I can truly relish that success. Other goals can naturally fall away because they're not important to me now, or something else has taken precedence.

RECOGNIZING ACCOMPLISHMENT

▶ Pioneering Psychologist Martin Seligman chose accomplishment as one of his 'five cornerstones of well-being' for a good reason. There is such a source of energy and sustenance available to you in recognizing your achievements. Reflecting on what is going well is a powerful way to boost your sense of self-worth. This is not just about public accolades and the big things like graduations – it is about noticing a job well done on an everyday level. Motherhood makes this crystal clear to me. When I get lost in the relentless nature of parenting, life feels like 'Groundhog Day'. Remembering to look out for a sense of achievement in the humdrum, I feel my spirits lift.

I think it is useful here to acknowledge that at different times in our life, success can mean different things and we need to adjust our definition of accomplishment so that it is appropriate to the roles and responsibilities we currently hold. Before kids, accomplishment in my career was really tangible. I had clients verbally expressing their thanks for my efforts, a fully booked work diary reminding me of my worth and bottles of wine at Christmas making me feel very valued. Parenthood? Different story. There are no pay rises or promotions. My 'client' rarely says thank you for a nappy change – in fact, most of the time I have to fight his opposition to getting the job done. How many teenagers thank you for stocking the fridge? Doing the dishes certainly doesn't fill me with a sense of making a valuable contribution to this world... but is there accomplishment? Damn right there is. We just need to train our eyes to see it.

We all need to learn how to give ourselves a pat on the back for knocking down the tasks in our day. When I recognize each mini accomplishment for the genuine achievement that it is there can be a feeling of genuine triumph in knowing my kids are clothed, fed and nurtured. Mums and dads, you are not just wiping noses or forever driving your child to their next engagement – zoom out and see that you are nurturing a human being!

Running your own business or working flat-out for a manager? Feedback and praise can be hard to come by. Maybe your working days are behind you and your sense of achievement needs to come from avenues other than employment. Be on the lookout for your accomplishments, small and large. Reflect on the effort you've put in to make them happen and savour that achievement. Feel how the act of noticing your accomplishments fills your cup! Don't just wait for others to say 'well done', you can do it for yourself and it can feel just as satisfying. I think it is a beautiful thing to make it a habit to recognize the achievements of others too. Feel that upward spiral of positivity bloom!

SAY HELLO TO YOUR FUTURE SELF!

▸ When I am working towards a goal and I find myself tempted by something that sabotages my long-term progress, the concept of 'past', 'present' and 'future' self is helpful. Your past self is the person you were yesterday, five years ago, twenty years ago. When it comes to goals, know that you can't change your past self, you can only change how you feel about it. Your present self is the person you are right now, in this moment, today. This is where your control lies – you have the power to effect who you are right now, your choices in this moment. Your future self is the person you are becoming, tomorrow, next month, in ten years' time. Your future self is the culmination of every decision your present self makes – I make better decisions when I consciously make that connection.

When faced with a decision that impacts on your goal, hold in your mind's eye how each choice affects the person you are becoming. Does the choice you're about to make support who you aspire to be? Relate this back to past decisions and the results of those actions – learn from those choices. Can you delay gratification in this moment to nurture your 'future' self, even if your 'present' self is crying out? Is there a way that you could find satisfaction in this moment that doesn't sabotage the person you aspire to be? Strike a balance between caring for your present self and your future self.

Meditate on your future self – who is this person you are becoming, allow them to have a voice and listen to them! Know that the decisions and choices are yours, and that by making better choices most of the time, you will get closer to becoming the person you want to be. I turn forty this year and there is nothing like a significant date, event or milestone birthday to give you a kick up the tush. I've spent a lot of time conjuring this image of who I want to be at forty. I can see her, hear her and feel her presence. I often find myself asking 'What would she do?' and I know that if I make the same choice, I am taking one step closer to being that kick-ass best version of myself.

It can take time to carve the path you want to be on, so be persistent, compassionate and, most importantly, be kind to yourself. Acknowledge if you need a little help realizing your vision. If this has been something you've wanted for a long time and what you're doing isn't working, then enlist some support. Equally, if this is new and you don't know how to tackle it – reach out for help.

little gems ▸

▸ Bring your goal to life by thinking about the specific actions it will take to make it happen. Start out small by breaking your goal down into milestones you can celebrate. Proactively consider any obstacles and come up with solutions so it's easier to stay on course. Make a psychological contract with yourself and draw on the support of your team.

▸ You'll know if you've nailed your goal setting if it fills you with a sense of excitement.

▸ The best goals are based on what you find personally rewarding, are framed positively and tap into your values. Make sure there is some fluidity around your goals, taking into consideration your available time, energy and resources, and avoid setting goals that conflict with each other.

▸ Knowing how to formulate effective goals will help you create healthy new habits and is an essential step in making the commitment to any of the Vitality Wheel self-care activities.

▸ Get into the right frame of mind before brainstorming your goals by talking with a friend or boosting your creativity with a bout of uplifting exercise.

▸ Use your Vitality Journal and dream away without limiting yourself by needing to know how you will achieve it.

goal-setting & accomplishment

▶ Recognizing your accomplishments is a powerful self-care activity that boosts your self-esteem. Use your Vitality Journal to track your progress. Write down what went well in your day and bask in the simple pleasure of it.

▶ Spend some time thinking about what success means to you and acknowledge this is an evolving concept through different chapters of your life. Learn how to give yourself a pat on the back.

▶ Beat self-sabotage by thinking about the person you are becoming. Your 'future self' is the culmination of every choice you make in this moment. Remember you do have a choice, and by delaying gratification and making good choices most of the time you are moving closer to being the best version of yourself. Spend time in your Vitality Journal reflecting on who you aspire to be, let them have a voice, listen to them and become them one choice at a time.

▶ Goals fire up your motivation, give you grit, channel your attention and help you manage your time. They can also boost your happiness, so setting a goal is a self-care activity in itself.

YOGA TO BOOST YOUR FOCUS & MOTIVATION

Half sun salute

Stand feet hip-width apart and your hands on your outer
thighs. Inhale and reach your arms out and up, looking up.
Exhale and hinging at your hips, bend your knees, lower your
chest towards your thighs and your head towards your feet.
Inhale and bring your spine parallel to the floor, your hands
flat onto your shins, feeling the muscles of your back engage.
Exhale and relax back down into the fold. Inhale and slowly
rise back to upright with your arms above your head, looking
up. Exhale and bend your knees and sink into a squat with
your arms straight out in front of you. Inhale and return to
standing upright, arms overhead. Exhale and lower your arms
down and gaze forwards. Repeat 3–6 times to heat and
energize your body.

Warrior side lunge

Face sideways along your mat, with your feet twice shoulder-width apart. Turn your right toes out and press your left heel away to 45 degrees. Keeping your legs straight, breathe in and reach your arms above your head, palms touching and look up. As you breathe out, bend your right knee deeply and firmly straighten your left leg, stretching your arms out level with your shoulders. Repeat this 3–6 times before holding the lunge for 5 breaths and then changing legs.

Narrow standing fold

Stand feet hip-width apart, hinge at your hips and drape your upper body forwards along your thighs. Bring your fingertips to the floor and generously bend your knees, or if it feels good, work your legs straight. Be careful not to round your upper back. Allow your upper body to flop like a ragdoll and feel the crown of your head sink towards the floor. Stay here for 5–10 breaths before slowly rolling your way back to upright.

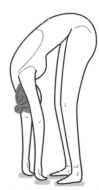

eight

VALUES & PURPOSE

▸ You could call 2014 my year of digging deep. We made bold decisions and big moves, and despite our optimism, it was like wading through treacle. But I would do it all again in a heartbeat! There's nothing more precious to me than time with a loved one, or a parent meeting their grandchild, or seeing your partner flourish. However, it hasn't been easy and there have been many lessons learnt.

Here's a snapshot: While pregnant, we sold our first flat, prepared the family home of forty years for sale, said goodbye to our Sydney life and moved to the UK. We lived out of a suitcase for four months, worked hard on creating career opportunities, had a baby and settled our daughter into her first school. The year was book-ended by a family Christmas with all of my husband's family and the very sad, but expected, passing of my dear father-in-law.

It was a challenging and often lonely time, but dotted with some real peak experiences. On reflection, knowing why saw me through. When all else failed, knowing that there was a solid reason behind our choices made it easier to keep on. It was a tool that enabled me to see beyond just myself and my ego, and to keep connected with the bigger picture. Every time I found a trickle of doubt enter my head about our move I reminded myself that this was about having time with Dave's father. Feeling that we were acting from the heart and taking action guided by our values allowed me to have faith in our path.

Taking leaps of faith guided by principles can seem the straightforward thing to do, but don't then expect it to be easy! Sometimes when we set ourselves on a courageous, values-driven course we can become impatient. I remember feeling frustrated when things weren't unfolding as we had planned. The right jobs were harder to come by than expected, we didn't get the school place we really hoped for, we missed out on three houses... at the time I felt like the universe should have been conspiring to make things possible because we were doing the 'right' thing. We had been clear on our values, we had taken purposeful action and still the desired results were not forthcoming... in the timeframes I wanted. This is an important distinction to make. The fruits of our labour came, but it took far longer and involved more hard work and heartache than I expected. The mantra I like to use to access patience and optimism is 'It is coming'. When that feeling of 'I want it yesterday' creeps up on me or when my objectives are a million miles away, repeating those words calms me down.

Getting in touch with your values is the magic ingredient that brings all the different parts of the Vitality Wheel together. Your values lie at the heart of why you engage in self-care, and by committing to regular self-care you are in the best possible place to live the life that you aspire to lead and to become the person you aspire to be. So for me, it is to be the kind of patient, loving and compassionate mum I aspire to be, to work professionally with strength and authenticity, to be the kind of partner I aspire to be and to enjoy the kind of marriage I hold dear. Self-care is a dual feedback loop – you engage in self-care to fully live your values, and articulating your values will motivate you to commit to self-care.

Connecting with your purpose can transform how you feel about an activity, role in life or your circumstances. When you evaluate your choices in light of what takes you towards or away from your values, it gives you clarity on the right path of action and decision making gets easier. It's not enough to know what you want in life – you've got to know why you want it. Being really crystal clear on why you are taking a particular course of action galvanizes you to keep going when life tests you.

Getting connected with your values is a sure-fire way to feel invigorated and inspired, and that's why just thinking about your values is a self-care activity. When you take action in service of those values you tap into a feeling of authenticity, and that's the quality that helps you step up in the face of challenge.

Getting in touch with your values is the magic ingredient that brings all the different parts of the Vitality Wheel together.

UNDERSTANDING YOUR VALUES

HOW ARE VALUES DIFFERENT TO GOALS?

▸ Values are personally chosen life directions, the guiding principles with no end point that shape and define our lives, whereas goals are something that can be finished or accomplished. Your goals give you focus and determination; your values clarity and purpose. We set goals in service of our values. Values tap into what really matters to us as individuals, and what we perceive a well-lived life to look like. Talking about, thinking about and acting in service of values will ignite a powerful feeling of energy.

DEFINING WITH YOUR VALUES

▸ Listed opposite are some points for reflection. Use any of these questions as inspiration for clarifying your values. Think about it, meditate on it, talk about it with friends, jot down your reflections in your Vitality Journal or create a vision board. You can make it as visual as you want by writing down or clipping from magazines any key words, affirmations or slogans that resonate for you. My fridge has become a vision board of sorts – photos, my daughter's school awards, my holiday wishlist in images and post-it notes with motivating words. You could equally use your Vitality Journal. Have fun with it.

Who do you aspire to be?

My favourite way of bringing values to life is thinking about the various roles I play every day. Ask yourself what qualities do you aspire to possess in the roles you play or how would you like to be remembered? How do you want to be as a partner, as a parent, as a daughter or son, as a friend or in the workplace?

What virtues are important to you?

Another of my favourite ways to get clear on what you care about and what you naturally do well draws on the work of psychologists Dr Martin Seligman and Dr Chris Peterson, who created the 'Values in Action, Inventory of Strengths' test. You can take it online or use the list of twenty-four character strengths as food for thought. They are: creativity or ingenuity, curiosity or interest in the world, critical thinking or open-mindedness, love of learning, perspective, bravery, perseverance or diligence, honesty or integrity, zest or passion, the capacity to love and be loved, kindness, social intelligence, loyalty or teamwork, fairness and equity, leadership, forgiveness, humility, prudence or caution, self-control, appreciation of beauty and excellence, gratitude, hope, humour, spirituality or faith. From this list, what qualities do you aspire to develop and actively role model?

The survey is available free of charge at www.viacharacter.org/www/Character-Strengths-Survey. Once you've finished, you'll be given a ranking of the 24 strengths. Pay attention to the top five, your strengths, and if you're interested think of the bottom five as areas for improvement. Look for ways that you can put your strengths to good use and notice how this energizes you.

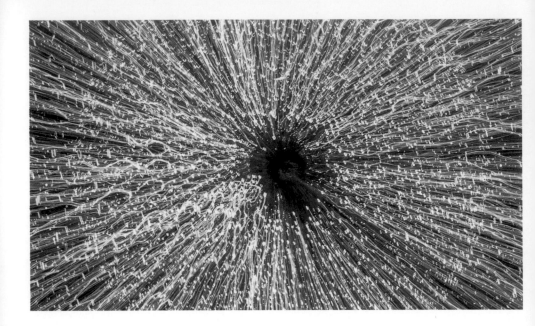

What inspires awe or anger?

Think of a situation or issue that makes you angry or outraged. Consider why this makes you angry. What principle does this situation compromise or impinge? Conversely, reflect on a person you admire. What does this person stand for, what did they contribute or what is it about them that you hold in such esteem? These are the qualities and beliefs that you value.

What's on your bucket list?

Have you made a list of all the precious things you'd like to achieve or experience before you conk out? Asking yourself why you want these things can be fertile ground for articulating what's most important to you. Or ponder the question, 'If I had thirty days to live I would...' to crystalize what you hold dear in life.

CREATING BALANCE IN LIFE

▸ Think about the different aspects of your life including love, family and friends, work, health, personal growth and education, recreation, finance and standard of living, community, spiritual life, or physical environment. What is personally meaningful to you in those different spheres and what are the actions you could take to grow and develop? This can be deeply nourishing, so add these actions to your Self-Care Toolkit if you feel inspired by them.

It helps to create some kind of balance in the energy we put into these different aspects of life. Sometimes when I feel pressure around my work life, I plough too much energy into it at the expense of other facets of my life. What I have found is that by addressing these other areas – like investing in my social bonds or even simply getting on top of my domestic tasks – I am creating a shift in energy. The blockage is removed and things start to blossom on the career front even though I have been attending to other valuable pursuits.

BRINGING YOUR PURPOSE TO LIFE

▸ Once you're clear on your values look for ways that you can put them into action. Being of service to others is a way of taking these ideas off the page and breathing life into them. Watch what happens when you dedicate your energy and effort to something greater than yourself. This is the mantra I often use at the end of my daily meditation: 'All that I am, I offer up in service of all humanity and for all that I receive I am truly thankful'. If this resonates for you, spend some time contemplating it and find ways to bring it into action.

This point also emphasizes that we are not living in a bubble – we are individuals operating in relation to the people around us and there is a sense of timing to how opportunities unfold. I think there are chapters in life where it feels like it is your 'turn' and other times in your life when you take a back seat. We need to keep our perspective rooted in the larger context – it's not just about us. There are other people in our life to consider, there are other aspirations at play. Can we be generous and let someone else have a turn without begrudging them their time in the sun. Ours will come, it may just not be when we expect it.

VALUES & THE VITALITY WHEEL

▶ Open up your Vitality Journal and jot down each
  spoke of the Vitality Wheel that you feel drawn to
  working with. Tap into your values by asking yourself
  what does this kind of nourishment facilitate you to
  do or be? You could create some form of mission
  statement if you like – essentially you are stating your
  'why' and this acts as a primer statement for that
  behaviour. You'll see that's how I designed a few of
  my mantras! There's no right or wrong here, and there
  may be several for each spoke of the Vitality Wheel.
  Overleaf are some examples to get you thinking.

When I exercise, I deal better with stress and am a nicer person. (Move for mental health.)

When I prioritize sleep, I am more patient and compassionate. (Sleep for sanity.)

Making time for laughter and fun with my family strengthens our bonds. (The family that plays together stays together.)

When I talk to myself with kindness I am kinder to others also. (Only talk to yourself as you would your best friend.)

notes to myself ›

little gems ‣

‣ It is a dual feedback loop between self-care and knowing our values: we nourish ourselves with self-care so that we can lead a well-lived life and be the best version of ourselves. Clarify your values and you'll be motivated to engage in active self-care, diminishing guilt around taking time for yourself.

‣ Seek balance in your life and look at the flow of energy you direct between the different aspects of your life. Balance your activity between nurturing love, family and friends, work, health, personal growth and education, fun and recreation, finance and standard of living, community, spiritual life, or physical environment.

‣ Determine your values by reflecting on, writing about or gathering images inspired by the following questions: Who do you aspire to be in the different roles you play in life? What qualities do you care about? What inspires awe or makes you angry? What's on your bucket list and why?

‣ If you feel impatient, remind yourself 'it is coming' and consider the concept of turn taking in your close relationships.

▸ Values are the qualities that matter to you, the things in life you care deeply about. Think of values as life directions that can never be crossed off whereas we set goals that can be completed, in service to our values.

▸ To make the commitment to engaging in self-care, ask yourself what each spoke of the Vitality Wheel facilitates you to do or be. Write out your own mantras or mission statements in your Vitality Journal and feel how nourishing yourself is the ultimate win-win.

▸ Getting clear on your purpose has the potential to spark great joy, motivation and firm resolve. What's your why? Have you embarked on a bold course of action – a project, a business venture, a new chapter in life or family commitments? Or are you setting out to make one tiny change in your daily behaviour with a new healthy habit? Take a moment to reflect on why you are doing it and write it down in your Vitality Journal. In tough times, remind yourself of this bigger picture and it'll help you through.

▸ Bring your values to life by being of service to others. Try the mantra: 'All that I am, I offer up in service of all humanity and for all that I receive I am truly thankful'.

YOGA TO CONNECT YOU WITH YOUR HEART & TO CHANNEL YOUR RESOLVE

Supine, alternating knee hugs

Lie down on your mat, stretching your legs out, with your arms down by your sides. Inhale and reach your arms up and overhead. Exhale and hug your right knee into your chest holding on with both hands. Inhale to stretch your arms overhead again and lower the right leg back to the floor. Exhale to hug your left knee into your chest. Your heels remain flexed throughout to activate your legs. Repeat 6 times on each leg. Be prepared to let go along the way, blowing away what you no longer need.

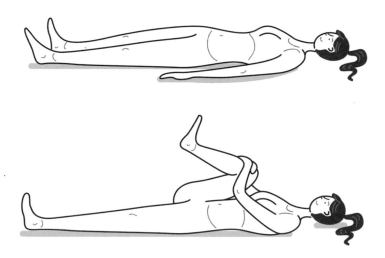

Basic twist

Draw your knees into your chest and take your arms out wide by your sides at shoulder height. Bring your knees over towards your right elbow and relax your legs and feet completely down to the floor. Hold onto the top knee with your right hand to anchor your legs. Gaze towards the left and hold for 5–10 breaths, consciously letting gravity do the work for you. Just surrender and let go. Repeat to the other side.

Reclining butterfly pose

Lie on the floor with a bolster underneath your knees or a cushion underneath each knee. Bring the soles of your feet together and let your knees drop into the support beneath them. Gently rest your fingertips on your belly, breathing into your stomach. Close your eyes. Completely soften your body and feel your hands rise and fall with your breath for 5–10 minutes. Relax, have faith, everything you need to achieve your goals is within you already. Feel it deeply within you and allow that to lead you out into the rest of your day. Well done.

YOUR SELF-CARE TOOLKIT

▶ Sit and breathe. Give yourself a mental pat on the back for investing in yourself and taking in lots of life-giving information. This is active self-care and the next step is to take action. Reflect on the person that you aspire to be and recognize that your commitment to self-care is the means by which you become this 'best self' – there is nothing selfish about that, in fact consider how all your loved ones benefit.

Brené Brown sums it up perfectly saying, 'be the adult you want your children to be'[45]. If you don't have children, then be the adult you wanted your parents to be. What this means to each of us varies, but for me, I want my kids to have a positive relationship with self-care and to have plenty of resources to sustain them through life's challenges. The best way I can teach them is to engage actively in self-care myself, involve them in the process and teach them its value. I also want to raise resilient, kind and diligent human beings, and they need to know how to nourish themselves to be this best expression of themselves. If these are the qualities I want them to value, I have to role model them and I can only be that person when I am tending to my energetic bank balance with self-care. And it's not just relevant for parents, this holds for any relationship. If you want the people surrounding you to be kind and patient, the best start is being kind and patient yourself.

WHAT TO DO NEXT

▸ Be proactive – revisit the Vitality Wheel and make it your own. Write down several self-care activities inspired by each pathway of the Vitality Wheel. Use your notes to create your own Self-Care Toolkit and keep it to hand for easy reference. You can either simply list all the self-care activities that appeal to you now or you could try one of my favourite ways of bringing self-care to life by generating a list of mood states and writing down what you'll do to help yourself in that circumstance. Write out your statements in the form of 'If I am feeling X, then I will do Y'.

This is active self-care and the next step is to take action.

So for example, my Self-Care Toolkit at the moment looks something like this:

If I am feeling low, then I will use my Vitality Journal to reflect on my goals.

If I am feeling fatigued, then I will stand up tall and take six mountain breaths.

If I am feeling time poor,
then I will repeat:
'I have all the time I need'.

If I am feeling anxious, then I will smooth out my breathing and relax any physical tension I find.

If I am feeling lonely, then I will scan through who's on my team and reach out to someone.

If I am feeling reactive, then I will seek out nature and take a moment to enjoy its beauty.

If I am feeling scattered, then I will focus on my personal 'why'.

If I am feeling bored, then I will think about something I am looking forward to.

If I am feeling fed up, then I will take a walk around the block to let off steam.

If I am feeling frustrated with someone I love, then I will zoom in on their captivating qualities.

If I am feeling happy, then I will savour it!

This list isn't exhaustive but it helps me cut through the mental chatter, the inertia and do something constructive. The reason why I like this strategy so much is that each statement feels like a commitment I've made to myself. Reading through this list in times of need vastly increases the likelihood of me engaging in a life-giving behaviour rather than floundering around in an emotional reaction that potentially sabotages my goals. I am sure this will help you better navigate times of stress too.

MAKING TIME FOR SELF-CARE

▶ If it resonates for you, make an appointment with yourself and plan which self-care activity you are going to enjoy. In moments of stress, refer to your annotated Vitality Wheel or Self-Care Toolkit and choose something that will help you cope better. When you have a spare moment, use these resources to choose a life-giving activity so you don't fritter away an opportunity to fill your cup. You will need to keep coming back to this book to keep your commitment fresh and your motivation strong – be prepared for that. Keep your Self-Care Toolkit evolving for maximal impact. I hope you enjoy exploring yoga too!

If you enjoy the process of writing, revisit your Vitality Journal and take a look at the goals you set for yourself earlier. Would you like to amend them or set new ones? If you haven't set goals yet, are you ready to make a psychological contract with yourself now? Can you define three action steps towards achieving your goals and some loose timeframes around them? Is there something you can do now? Why wait!

SELF-CARE ISN'T SELFISH!

▶ And when that gremlin raises its head saying 'this is indulgent', 'you don't have the time or energy', shake it off with a smile. Those self-limiting beliefs are simply not the truth. If you're in the midst of stress and feel tempted to put self-care in the 'too hard basket', please don't – this is precisely the time you need it the most and it will help you to keep going. Rebuilding your energy stores with self-care after a period of challenge, change or grief is not extravagant, it's the means by which you get back on your feet. Keeping yourself energetically topped up to avoid being floored by the inevitable curveballs of life is not a luxury – it's sensible, wise and necessary. Nourishing yourself head, heart and body so that you can be the kind of person you want to be for you and everyone around you is not an indulgence. There is time! There are ways of nurturing yourself that don't require any energy or effort. Just open your eyes and own it.

Thank you so much for coming on this journey with me. I hope you feel kitted up and inspired with ways to take care of yourself: physically, emotionally, energetically and mentally. While much of this is common sense, in truth it can be hard to implement. So go slowly and gently. Don't let your self-care routine become yet another item on your to-do list. If you fall short of your intentions, don't berate yourself. Keep remembering your personal 'why'. Most importantly, keep taking action. You deserve to flourish and the only person that can really do something about it is you. We are in it together.

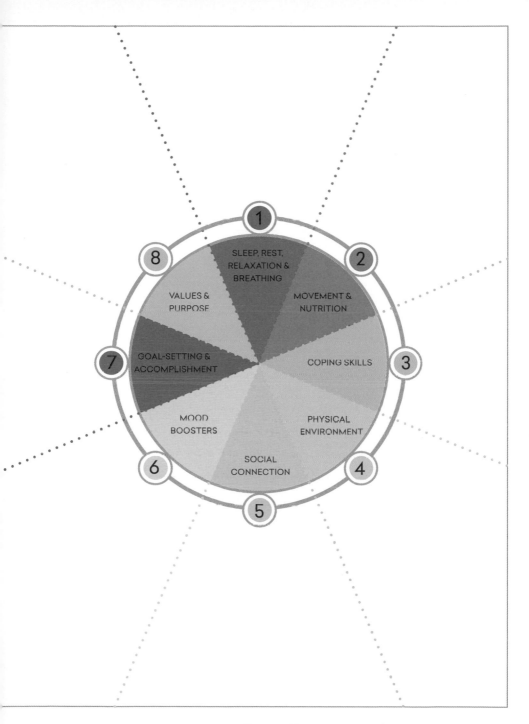

MANTRAS AND AFFIRMATIONS

Self-care is health care.

Self-care isn't selfish.

Self-care: it's not me first, it's me AS WELL.

 Sleep for sanity.

Does this REALLY need to be done right now?

It is just time for me to rest.

There is nothing required of me right now.

If I can't sleep, then I will rest. If I can't slow my mind, then I will soften my body. I receive the inhalation, I surrender to the exhalation. I become my breath.

I release what I no longer need, I let go of what no longer serves me.

 Move for mental health.

Eat like a sparrow and you get a bird's brain.

If I am going to indulge, then I will savour it.

 I soften into this moment.

I give myself permission to...

Put a ring around it.

Can I do anything about this?

Don't believe everything you think!

What's the silver lining here?

Will this matter in a year?

I have all the time I need.

Tidy house, tidy mind.

I feel the support of the earth beneath me.

I allow my body to be held by the earth.

I am safe, I am loved, I am held.

I am radiant love.

Hurt people hurt people.

Above all, be kind.

Don't be THE bigger person, be A bigger person.

We're in it together.

This is time just to enjoy, everything else can wait.

Look up!

My day can begin again in any moment.

I am already enough. I am already whole. I am already perfect. There is no hole to fill, nothing to fix, nothing to be done.

I fire my arrow of intent.

The universe supports me and my intention.

I am resolute, nothing will blow me off course.

Everything I need to achieve my aspirations is within me already.

I appreciate me.

All that I am, I offer up in service of all humanity and for all that I receive I am truly thankful.

What have I contributed today?

I take action in service of my values.

It is coming!

REFERENCES

[1] World Health Organisation Executive Board, 'Global burden of mental disorders and the need for a comprehensive, coordinated response from health and social sectors at the country level'. EB130/9 130th session 1 December 2011. Provisional agenda item 6.2

[2] Frederick, S., and Loewenstein, G., 'Hedonic adaptation' in D. Kahneman and E. Deiner, and N. Schwarz (Eds.), *Wellbeing: The foundations of hedonic psychology*, (New York: Russell Sage Foundation, 1999), 302–329,

[3] Falsafi, N. 'A Randomized Controlled Trial of Mindfulness Versus Yoga: Effects on Depression and/or Anxiety in College Students', *Journal of the American Psychiatric Nurses Association* (Aug 26, 2016)

[4] De Manincor, M., Bensoussan, A., Smith, C., Barr, K., Schweickle, M., Donoghoe, L., Bourchier, S., and Fahey, P., 'Individualised yoga for reducing depression and anxiety, and improving well-being: a randomized controlled trial', *Depression and Anxiety*, (2016), 1–13

[5] Bhatia T, Mazumdar S, Wood J, He F, Gur RE, Gur RC, Nimgaonkar VL, Deshpande SN. 'A randomised controlled trial of adjunctive yoga and adjunctive physical exercise training for cognitive dysfunction in schizophrenia', *Acta Neuropsychiatrica*, 12 (2016 Aug), 1–13

[6] Chaturvedi, A., Nayak, G., Nayak, A.G., Rao, A. 'Comparative Assessment of the Effects of Hatha Yoga and Physical Exercise on Biochemical Functions in Perimenopausal Women', *Journal of Clinical and Diagnostic Research*, 10 (Aug 2016), 8

[7] Rhodes, A., Spinazzola, J., van der Kolk, B. 'Yoga for Adult Women with Chronic PTSD: A Long-Term Follow-Up Study', *Journal of Alternative Complementary Medicine*, 22 (3) (Mar 2016), 189–96

[8] Yadav, R.1, Yadav, R.K., Khadgawat, R., Mehta, N. 'Beneficial Effects of a 12-Week Yoga-Based Lifestyle Intervention on Cardio-Metabolic Risk Factors and Adipokines in Subjects with Pre-Hypertension or Hypertension', J Hypertens, 34 (Sep 2016), Suppl 1

[9] Chu, P., Pandya, A., Salomon, J.A., Goldie SJ, Hunink MG. 'Comparative Effectiveness of Personalized Lifestyle Management Strategies for Cardiovascular Disease Risk Reduction', *Journal of the American Heart Association*, 5 (3) (29 Mar 2016), e002737

[10] Frank, R., Larimore,, J. 'Yoga as a method of symptom management in multiple sclerosis', *Frontiers of Neuroscience*, 9 (2015), 133

[11] Sharma, M., Lingam, V.C., Nahar, V.K. 'A systematic review of yoga interventions as integrative treatment in breast cancer', J Cancer Res Clin Oncol, 15 (Sep 2016)

[12] Cheung, C., Park, J., Wyman, J.F. 'Effects of Yoga on Symptoms, Physical Function, and Psychosocial Outcomes in Adults with Osteoarthritis: A Focused Review', *American Journal of Physical Medicine and Rehabilitation*, 95 (2) (Feb 2016), 139–51

[13] Satish, L., Lakshmi, V.S. 'Impact of individualized yoga therapy on perceived quality of life performance on cognitive tasks and depression among Type II diabetic patients', *International Journal of Yoga*, 9 (2) (Jul–Dec 2016), 130–6

[14] Wang, F.1, Eun-Kyoung Lee, O.2, Feng, F.1, Vitiello, M.V.3, Wang, W.4, Benson, H.5, Fricchione, G.L.5, Denninger, J.W.5 'The effect of meditative movement on sleep quality: A systematic review', *Sleep Medicine Reviews*, 30 (12 Dec 2015), 43–52

[15] Ross, A., Brooks, A., Touchton-Leonard, K., and Wallen, G. 'A Different Weight Loss Experience: A Qualitative Study Exploring the Behavioural, Physical, and Psychosocial Changes Associated with Yoga That Promote Weight Loss', *Evidence Based Complementary Alternative Medicine*, (2016), 2914745.

[16] Motorwala, Z.S.1, Kolke, S.1, Panchal, P.Y.1, Bedekar, N.S.1, Sancheti, P.K.2, Shyam, A.2. 'Effects of Yoga asanas on osteoporosis in postmenopausal women', *International Journal of Yoga*, 9 (1) (Jan–Jul 2016), 44–8

[17] UK Sleep Council 'Great British Bedtime Report 2013'

[18] Van Dongen, H. P., Maislin, G., Muligan, J. M., and Dinges, D, F., 'The Cumulative Cost of Additional Wakefulness: Dose-Response Effects on Neurobehavioral Functions and Sleep Physiology from Chronic Sleep Restriction and Total Sleep Deprivation,' *Sleep*, 26 (2003), 117–26.

[19] Williamson, A. M., and Feyer, A., 'Moderate Sleep Deprivation Produces Impairments in Cognitive and Motor Performance Equivalent to Legally Prescribed Levels of Alcohol Intoxication', *Occupational & Environmental Medicine* 57, 649 (2000), 55

[20] Chang, A.M., Aeschbach, D., Duffy, J.F., Czeisler, C.A. 'Evening use of light-emitting eReaders negatively affects sleep, circadian timing, and next-morning alertness', *Proceedings of the National Academy of Sciences USA*, 112 (2015), 1232–7.

[21] Seligman, M. *Flourish: A Visionary New Understanding of Happiness and Well-being*, (New York: Free Press 2011), 33–4

[22] Chen, N., Xia, X., Qin, L., Luo, L., Han, S., Wang, G., Zhang, R., Wan, Z. 'Effects of 8-Week Hatha Yoga Training on Metabolic and Inflammatory Markers in Healthy, Female Chinese Subjects: A Randomized Clinical Trial', *Biomed Research International*, vol. 2016 (2016), Article ID 5387258, 12 pages

[23] Singleton, O., Hölzel, B.K., Vangel, M., Brach, N., Carmody, J., Lazar, S.W. 'Change in Brainstem Gray Matter Concentration Following a Mindfulness-Based Intervention is Correlated with Improvement in Psychological Well-Being', *Frontiers in Human Neuroscience*, 8 (18 Feb 2014), 33

[24] Rani, K., Tiwari, S., Singh, U., Agrawal, G., Ghildiyal, A., Srivastava, N. 'Impact of Yoga Nidra on psychological general well-being in patients with menstrual irregularities: A randomized controlled trial.' *International Journal of Yoga*, 4 (1) (Jan–Jun 2011), 20–5.

[25] Lark, L., Goullet, T. *Healing Yoga*, (London: Carlton Books, 2005)

[26] Seppala, E. M., Nitschke, J. B., Tudorascu, D. L., Hayes, A., Goldstein, M. R., Nguyen, D. T. H., Perlman, D., Davidson, R. J. 'Breathing-based meditation decreases post-traumatic stress disorder symptoms in military veterans: A randomized controlled longitudinal study', *Journal of Traumatic Stress*, Volume 27, Issue 4 (August 2014), 397–405

[27] Gollwitzer, P. 'Implementation Intentions: Strong Effects of Simple Plans', *American Psychologist*, 54, no. 7 (1999), 493–503

[28] Crum, Alia J., Langer, Ellen J. 'Mind-set matters: Exercise and the placebo effect', *Psychological Science*, 18, no. 2 (2007), 165–171.

[29] http://gretchenrubin.com/happiness_project/2012/10/back-by-popular-demand-are-you-an-abstainer-or-a-moderator/

[30] Lyubomirsky, S., and Tkach, C., 'The consequences of dysphoric rumination', in C. Papageorgiou and A. Wells (Eds.), *Rumination: Nature, theory, and treatment of negative thinking in depression*, (Chichester, England: John Wiley and Sons, 2003), 21–41

[31] Tedeschi, R. G., & Calhoun, L. G., *Trauma and transformation: Growing in the aftermath of suffering*, (Thousand Oaks, CA: Sage, 1995)

[32] Peterson, C., Park, N., Pole, N., D'Andrea, W. & Seligman, M. *Journal of Traumatic Stress*, Vol. 21, No. 2 (April 2008), 214–217

[33] Walsh, R., 'Lifestyle and Mental Health', *American Psychologist*, Vol. 66, No. 7 (2011), 579–592

[34] Walsh, R., *Essential spirituality: The seven central practices*, (New York: Wiley, 1999)

[35] Kondo, M., *The Life Changing Magic of Tidying*, (London: Vermillion, 2011)

[36] Fredrickson, B. L., *Love 2.0 How Our Supreme Emotion Affects Everything We Fell, Think, Do and Become*, (New York: Hudson Street Press, 2013)

[37] Gable, S.L., Gonzaga, G.C., & Strachman, A., 'Will you be there for me when things go right? Supportive responses to positive event disclosures', *Journal of Personality and Social Psychology*, 91(5) (2006), 904–917

[38] Gottman, J. M., *What predicts divorce: The relationship between marital processes and marital outcomes*, (Hillsdale, NJ: Lawrence Erlbaum, 1994)

[39] Peper, E. & Lin, I., 'Increase or Decrease Depression: How Body Postures Influence Your Energy Level', *Biofeedback*, Volume 40, Issue 3 (2012), 125–130

[40] Lyubomirsky, S., *The How of Happiness*, (London: Piatkus, 2007)

[41] Adams Miller, C., Frisch, M., *Creating your best life: The Ultimate Life List Guide*, (New York: Sterling, 2009)

[42] Cantor, N., Sanderson, C. A., 'Life task participation and well-being: The importance of taking part in daily life', in D. Kahneman, E. Diener, and N. Schwarz (Eds.), *Well-being: The foundations of hedonic psychology*, (New York: Russell Sage Foundation, 1999), 230–243

[43] Lyubomirsky, S., *The How of Happiness*, (London: Piatkus, 2007).

[44] Logel, C., Cohen, G., 'The role of the self in physical health: testing the effect of a values-affirmation intervention on weight loss', *Psychological Science*, Vol. 23 (2013), 53–55.

[45] Kogan, J., 'Brené Brown: Be the adult you want your children to be', *The Washington Post*, (5 October 2012)

INDEX

You deserve to flourish
and the only person
that can really do
something about
it is you.

ACKNOWLEDGEMENTS

While self-care has been my tonic, the love and support of family and friends have truly seen me through. Endless thanks go to my husband Dave, who's walked every step of the last fourteen years with me; to my parents, who gave me every opportunity possible; and my brothers, Michael and Robert, for guiding and encouraging me. Thanks go to Helen, Kim, Shaz and Noelene for your hands-on help, always. My impeccable friends, Lani, Trent, Brett, Dawn, Jo, Brad, Asty, Mal, Sally and Karen – who lifted me up when life seemed impossibly heavy. To Amanda Hoy and Michael de Manincor, who have been instrumental in my healing journey. To Nikki, Charlotte and Donna for making a new place feel like home in no time. A debt of gratitude goes to my agent Jane Graham-Maw and to Kate Adams at Aster for this opportunity. I'm also indebted to Pauline Bache, my editor, and Abigail Read, my illustrator, for their responsiveness, creativity and fantastic effort. Charlotte and Teddy, thanks for your patience and giant hugs – you make everything worth it.

Picture credits